MASTER THE™ DSST®

Ethics in Technology Exam

About Peterson's

Peterson's® has been your trusted educational publisher for over 50 years. It's a milestone we're quite proud of, as we continue to offer the most accurate, dependable, high-quality educational content in the field, providing you with everything you need to succeed. No matter where you are on your academic or professional path, you can rely on Peterson's for its books, online information, expert test-prep tools, the most up-to-date education exploration data, and the highest quality career success resources—everything you need to achieve your education goals. For our complete line of products, visit **www.petersons.com**.

For more information, contact Peterson's, 4380 S. Syracuse Street, Suite 200, Denver CO 80237; 800-338-3282 Ext. 54229; or find us online at **www.petersons.com**.

ISBN: 978-0-7689-4447-1

Printed in the United States of America

10 9 8 7 6 5 4 3 2 1   23 22 21

Contents

Before You Begin

HOW THIS BOOK IS ORGANIZED

Peterson's *Master the*™ *DSST® Ethics in Technology Exam* provides a diagnostic test, subject-matter review, and a post-test.

- **Diagnostic Test**—Twenty multiple-choice questions, followed by an answer key with detailed answer explanations
- **Assessment Grid**—A chart designed to help you identify areas that you need to focus on based on your test results
- **Subject-Matter Review**—General overview of the exam subject, followed by a review of the relevant topics and terminology covered on the exam
- **Post-test**—Sixty multiple-choice questions, followed by an answer key and detailed answer explanations

The purpose of the diagnostic test is to help you figure out what you know—or don't know. The twenty multiple-choice questions are similar to the ones found on the DSST exam, and they should provide you with a good idea of what to expect. Once you take the diagnostic test, check your answers to see how you did. Included with each correct answer is a brief explanation regarding why a specific answer is correct, and in many cases, why other options are incorrect. Use the assessment grid to identify the questions you miss so that you can spend more time reviewing that information later. As with any exam, knowing your weak spots greatly improves your chances of success.

Following the diagnostic test is a subject-matter review. The review summarizes the various topics covered on the DSST exam. Key terms are defined; important concepts are explained; and when appropriate, examples are provided. As you read the review, some of the information may seem familiar while other information may seem foreign. Again, take note of the unfamiliar because that will most likely cause you problems on the actual exam.

After studying the subject-matter review, you should be ready for the post-test. The post-test contains sixty multiple-choice items, and it will serve as a dry run for the real DSST exam. There are complete answer explanations at the end of the test.

OTHER DSST® PRODUCTS BY PETERSON'S

Books, flashcards, practice tests, and videos available online at
www.petersons.com/testprep/dsst

- A History of the Vietnam War
- Art of the Western World
- Astronomy
- Business Mathematics
- Business Ethics and Society
- Civil War and Reconstruction
- Computing and Information Technology
- Criminal Justice
- Environmental Science
- Ethics in America
- Ethics in Technology
- Foundations of Education
- Fundamentals of College Algebra
- Fundamentals of Counseling
- Fundamentals of Cybersecurity
- General Anthropology
- Health and Human Development
- History of the Soviet Union
- Human Resource Management

- Introduction to Business
- Introduction to Geography
- Introduction to Geology
- Introduction to Law Enforcement
- Introduction to World Religions
- Lifespan Developmental Psychology
- Math for Liberal Arts
- Management Information Systems
- Money and Banking
- Organizational Behavior
- Personal Finance
- Principles of Advanced English Composition
- Principles of Finance
- Principles of Public Speaking
- Principles of Statistics
- Principles of Supervision
- Substance Abuse
- Technical Writing

Like what you see? Get unlimited access to Peterson's full catalog of DSST practice tests, instructional videos, flashcards and more for **75% off the first month!** Go to **www.petersons.com/testprep/dsst** and use coupon code **DSST2020** at checkout. Offer expires July 1, 2021.

Chapter 1

All About the DSST® Exam

WHAT IS DSST®?

Previously known as the DANTES Subject Standardized Tests, the DSST program provides the opportunity for individuals to earn college credit for what they have learned outside of the traditional classroom. Accepted or administered at more than 1,900 colleges and universities nationwide and approved by the American Council on Education (ACE), the DSST program enables individuals to use the knowledge they have acquired outside the classroom to accomplish their educational and professional goals.

WHY TAKE A DSST® EXAM?

DSST exams offer a way for you to save both time and money in your quest for a college education. Why enroll in a college course in a subject you already understand? For more than 30 years, the DSST program has offered the perfect solution for individuals who are knowledgeable in a specific subject and want to save both time and money. A passing score on a DSST exam provides physical evidence to universities of proficiency in a specific subject. More than 1,900 accredited and respected colleges and universities across the nation award undergraduate credit for passing scores on DSST exams. With the DSST program, individuals can shave months off the time it takes to earn a degree.

The DSST program offers numerous advantages for individuals in all stages of their educational development:

- Adult learners
- College students
- Military personnel

Adult learners desiring college degrees face unique circumstances—demanding work schedules, family responsibilities, and tight budgets. Yet adult learners also have years of valuable work experience that can frequently be applied toward a degree through the DSST program. For example, adult learners with on-the-job experience in business and management might be able to skip the Business 101 courses if they earn passing marks on DSST exams such as Introduction to Business and Principles of Supervision.

Adult learners can put their prior learning into action and move forward with more advanced course work. Adults who have never enrolled in a college course may feel a little uncertain about their abilities. If this describes your situation, then sign up for a DSST exam and see how you do. A passing score may be the boost you need to realize your dream of earning a degree. With family and work commitments, adult learners often feel they lack the time to attend college. The DSST program provides adult learners with the unique opportunity to work toward college degrees without the time constraints of semester-long course work. DSST exams take two hours or less to complete. In one weekend, you could earn credit for multiple college courses.

The DSST exams also benefit students who are already enrolled in a college or university. With college tuition costs on the rise, most students face financial challenges. The fee for each DSST exam starts at $85 (plus administration fees charged by some testing facilities)—significantly less than the $750 average cost of a 3-hour college class. Maximize tuition assistance by taking DSST exams for introductory or mandatory course work. Once you earn a passing score on a DSST exam, you are free to move on to higher-level course work in that subject matter, take desired electives, or focus on courses in a chosen major.

Not only do college students and adult learners profit from DSST exams, but military personnel reap the benefits as well. If you are a member of the armed services at home or abroad, you can initiate your post-military career by taking DSST exams in areas with which you have experience. Military personnel can gain credit anywhere in the world, thanks to the fact that almost all of the tests are available through the internet at designated testing locations. DSST testing facilities are located at more than 500 military installations, so service members on active duty can get a jump-start on a post-military career with the DSST program. As an additional incentive, DANTES (Defense Activity for Non-Traditional Education Support) provides funding for DSST test fees for eligible members of the military.

More than 30 subject-matter tests are available in the fields of Business, Humanities, Math, Physical Science, Social Sciences, and Technology.

Available DSST® Exams

Business	Social Sciences
Business Ethics and Society	A History of the Vietnam War
Business Mathematics	Art of the Western World
Computing and Information Technology	Criminal Justice
Human Resource Management	Foundations of Education
Introduction to Business	Fundamentals of Counseling
Management Information Systems	General Anthropology
Money and Banking	History of the Soviet Union
Organizational Behavior	Introduction to Geography
Personal Finance	Introduction to Law Enforcement
Principles of Finance	Lifespan Developmental Psychology
Principles of Supervision	Substance Abuse
	The Civil War and Reconstruction
Humanities	**Physical Sciences**
Ethics in America	Astronomy
Introduction to World Religions	Environmental Science
Principles of Advanced English	Health and Human Development
Composition	Introduction to Geology
Principles of Public Speaking	
Math	**Technology**
Fundamentals of College Algebra	Ethics in Technology
Math for Liberal Arts	Fundamentals of Cybersecurity
Principles of Statistics	Technical Writing

As you can see from the table, the DSST program covers a wide variety of subjects. However, it is important to ask two questions before registering for a DSST exam.

1. Which universities or colleges award credit for passing DSST exams?
2. Which DSST exams are the most relevant to my desired degree and my experience?

Knowing which universities offer DSST credit is important. In all likelihood, a college in your area awards credit for DSST exams, but find out before taking an exam by contacting the university directly. Then review the list of DSST exams to determine which ones are most relevant to the degree you are seeking and to your base of knowledge. Schedule an appointment with your college adviser to determine which exams best fit your degree program and which college courses the DSST exams can replace. Advisers should also be able to tell you the minimum score required on the DSST exam to receive university credit.

DSST® TEST CENTERS

You can find DSST testing locations in community colleges and universities across the country. Check the DSST website (**www.getcollegecredit. com**) for a location near you or contact your local college or university to find out if the school administers DSST exams. Keep in mind that some universities and colleges administer DSST exams only to enrolled students. DSST testing is available to men and women in the armed services at more than 500 military installations around the world.

HOW TO REGISTER FOR A DSST® EXAM

Once you have located a nearby DSST testing facility, you need to contact the testing center to find out the exam administration schedule. Many centers are set up to administer tests via the internet, while others use printed materials. Almost all DSST exams are available as online tests, but the method used depends on the testing center. The cost for each DSST exam starts at $85, and many testing locations charge a fee to cover their costs for administering the tests. Credit cards are the only accepted payment method for taking online DSST exams. Credit card, certified check, and money order are acceptable payment methods for paper-and-pencil tests.

Test takers are allotted two score reports—one mailed to them and another mailed to a designated college or university, if requested. Online tests generate unofficial scores at the end of the test session, while individuals taking paper tests must wait four to six weeks for score reports.

PREPARING FOR A DSST® EXAM

Even though you are knowledgeable in a certain subject matter, you should still prepare for the test to ensure you achieve the highest score possible. The first step in studying for a DSST exam is to find out what will be on the specific test you have chosen. Information regarding test content is located on the DSST fact sheets, which can be downloaded at no cost from **www.**

getcollegecredit.com. Each fact sheet outlines the topics covered on a sub-ject-matter test, as well as the approximate percentage assigned to each topic. For example, questions on the Ethics in Technology exam are dis-tributed in the following way: Cyberspace and Privacy—21%, Domestic and International Security—21%, Legal Issues in Cyberspace—21%, Tech-nological Innovation and Ethics—17%, and Professional Ethics—20%.

In addition to the breakdown of topics on a DSST exam, the fact sheet also lists recommended reference materials. If you do not own the recom-mended books, then check college bookstores. Avoid paying high prices for new textbooks by looking online for used textbooks. Don't panic if you are unable to locate a specific textbook listed on the fact sheet; the textbooks are merely recommendations. Instead, search for comparable books used in university courses on the specific subject. Current editions are ideal, and it is a good idea to use at least two references when studying for a DSST exam. Of course, the subject matter provided in this book will be a suffi-cient review for most test takers. However, if you need additional informa-tion, then it is a good idea to have some of the reference materials at your disposal when preparing for a DSST exam.

Fact sheets include other useful information in addition to a list of refer-ence materials and topics. Each fact sheet includes subject-specific sample questions like those you will encounter on the DSST exam. The sample questions provide an idea of the types of questions you can expect on the exam. Test questions are multiple-choice with one correct answer and three incorrect choices.

The fact sheet also includes information about the number of credit hours ACE has recommended be awarded by colleges for a passing DSST exam score. However, you should keep in mind that not all universities and col-leges adhere to the ACE recommendation for DSST credit hours. Some institutions require DSST exam scores higher than the minimum score recommended by ACE. Once you have acquired appropriate reference materials and you have the outline provided on the fact sheet, you are ready to start studying, which is where this book can help.

TEST DAY

After reviewing the material and taking practice tests, you are finally ready to take your DSST exam. Follow these tips for a successful test day experience.

1. **Arrive on time.** Not only is it courteous to arrive on time to the DSST testing facility, but it also allows plenty of time for you to take care of check-in procedures and settle into your surroundings.

2. **Bring identification.** DSST test facilities require that candidates bring a valid government-issued identification card with a current photo and signature. Acceptable forms of identification include a current driver's license, passport, military identification card, or state-issued identification card. Individuals who fail to bring proper identification to the DSST testing facility will not be allowed to take an exam.

3. **Bring the right supplies.** If your exam requires the use of a calculator, you may bring a calculator that meets the specifications. For paper-based exams, you may also bring No. 2 pencils with an eraser and black ballpoint pens. Regardless of the exam methodology, you are NOT allowed to bring reference or study materials, scratch paper, or electronics such as cell phones, personal handheld devices, cameras, alarm wrist watches, or tape recorders to the testing center.

4. **Take the test.** During the exam, take the time to read each question-and-answer option carefully. Eliminate the choices you know are incorrect to narrow the number of potential answers. If a question completely stumps you, take an educated guess and move on—remember that DSSTs are timed; you will have 2 hours to take the exam.

With the proper preparation, DSST exams will save you both time and money. So join the thousands of people who have already reaped the benefits of DSST exams and move closer than ever to your college degree.

ETHICS IN TECHNOLOGY EXAM FACTS

The DSST® Ethics in Technology exam consists of 100 multiple-choice questions that assess students for knowledge equivalent to that acquired in an Ethics in Technology course. The exam includes the following topics: Cyberspace and Privacy, Domestic and International Security, Legal Issues in Cyberspace, Technological Innovation and Ethics, and Professional Ethics.

Area or Course Equivalent: Ethics in Technology
Level: Lower-level baccalaureate
Amount of Credit: 3 Semester Hours
Minimum Score: 400
Source: https://www.getcollegecredit.com/wp-content/assets/factsheets/EthicsInTechnology.pdf

I. **Cyberspace and Privacy – 21 %**

    a. Privacy and Security in Cyberspace

    b. Individual Conduct in Cyberspace

    c. Sharing with Online Communities and Social Networking Services

    d. Government Surveillance

    e. Corporate Uses of Personal Data

II. **Domestic and International Security – 21 %**

    a. Domestic and International Regulations

    b. Collection and Use of Personal Data: National Security

    c. Hacking and Counter-Hacking

    d. Information Warfare

    e. Cyberterrorism

III. **Legal Issues in Cyberspace – 21 %**

    a. Free Speech Issues

    b. Privacy Legislation and Industry Self-Regulation

    c. Intellectual Property

    d. Lawful Access and Encryption

    e. Cybercrimes

IV. **Technological Innovation and Ethics – 17 %**

    a. Biotechnologies

    b. Internet of Things

    c. Robotics and Artificial Intelligence

    d. Autonomous Vehicles

    e. Social Justice Issues

V. Professional Ethics – 20 %

a. Moral Obligations, Legal Liability, and Accountability of Corporations

b. Moral Responsibilities of IT Professionals

c. The Role of the Press

d. Social Media—Positive Re-enforcement and Dissemination of Unfounded Information

e. Net Neutrality

Chapter 2

Ethics in Technology Diagnostic Test

DIAGNOSTIC TEST ANSWER SHEET

1. Ⓐ Ⓑ Ⓒ Ⓓ
2. Ⓐ Ⓑ Ⓒ Ⓓ
3. Ⓐ Ⓑ Ⓒ Ⓓ
4. Ⓐ Ⓑ Ⓒ Ⓓ
5. Ⓐ Ⓑ Ⓒ Ⓓ
6. Ⓐ Ⓑ Ⓒ Ⓓ
7. Ⓐ Ⓑ Ⓒ Ⓓ

8. Ⓐ Ⓑ Ⓒ Ⓓ
9. Ⓐ Ⓑ Ⓒ Ⓓ
10. Ⓐ Ⓑ Ⓒ Ⓓ
11. Ⓐ Ⓑ Ⓒ Ⓓ
12. Ⓐ Ⓑ Ⓒ Ⓓ
13. Ⓐ Ⓑ Ⓒ Ⓓ
14. Ⓐ Ⓑ Ⓒ Ⓓ

15. Ⓐ Ⓑ Ⓒ Ⓓ
16. Ⓐ Ⓑ Ⓒ Ⓓ
17. Ⓐ Ⓑ Ⓒ Ⓓ
18. Ⓐ Ⓑ Ⓒ Ⓓ
19. Ⓐ Ⓑ Ⓒ Ⓓ
20. Ⓐ Ⓑ Ⓒ Ⓓ

ETHICS IN TECHNOLOGY DIAGNOSTIC TEST

24 minutes—20 questions

Directions: Carefully read each of the following 20 questions. Choose the best answer to each question and fill in the corresponding circle on the answer sheet. The Answer Key and Explanations can be found following this Diagnostic Test.

---

1. Supporters of net neutrality argue that ISPs should not be able to block content or prioritize services, and that

    A. providing tiered service levels will give small companies an advantage.
    B. providing tiered service levels will give large companies an advantage.
    C. ISPs and other service providers will be able to improve infrastructure.
    D. services that use massive amounts of data (e.g., Netflix, Skype, YouTube) should have to shoulder more of the financial burden.

2. The number one cybersecurity risk for organizations is

    A. human error.
    B. targeted ransomware attacks.
    C. hackers breaking through the organization's firewalls.
    D. DDoS (distributed denial of service) attacks.

3. The General Data Protection Regulation (GDPR) laws are seen by many businesses in the United States as

    A. too lax.
    B. too restrictive.
    C. not relevant to them.
    D. too narrow.

4. Augmented reality (AR) provides an interactive experience in which

    A. users "live" in a virtual world and interact with virtual beings.
    B. gamers can play with thousands of other gamers in real time.
    C. real-world objects are "enhanced" by computer-aided or computer-generated information.
    D. pilots see their instruments and other readouts on a mid-air display.

5. The ethical issue with political bots is not that they send out positive information about candidates, it's that they

  A. take advantage of a technology to which less popular candidates do not have access.

  B. often deceive candidates and staffers into retweeting what turns out to be false information.

  C. almost always generate what turn out to be false and malicious tweets.

  D. were not anticipated by the Founding Fathers and therefore should not have a place in elections.

6. Cyber-related legal issues relating to copyright, patents, trademarks, and trade secrets are said to involve what sort of property?

  A. Real property

  B. Commercial property

  C. Collective property

  D. Intellectual property

7. When "mainframe" computers were invented in the 1940s and 1950s, data security was not much of an issue because

  A. no one stored personal data on the computers.

  B. unlike today, computers then were not connected to one another.

  C. computer security was taken more seriously then.

  D. computers then were too large to break into.

8. In 2016, Facebook responded to criticisms that the platform was being used to spread false news items and hoaxes by unveiling a program designed to mitigate that problem. Among other steps taken, the company said that the new program would include all of the following features EXCEPT:

  A. Users can click on the upper-right corner of a post to indicate the post was a hoax.

  B. It would now be possible to flag posts as "disputed."

  C. The program will report spammers and scammers to the appropriate authorities.

  D. The company would work with third-party fact-checking organizations.

9. A "lawful access" mandate is a law that

A. protects one's encrypted data from being seized and decrypted by law enforcement or intelligence agencies.

B. gives law enforcement or intelligence agencies the power to access and decrypt encrypted data.

C. requires law enforcement or intelligence agencies to request data access from the creator or recipient of that data.

D. employs a mechanism that automatically destroys data if it is being sought by a law enforcement or intelligence agency.

10. The use of the internet to conduct violent acts that result in physical harm in order to achieve political or ideological gains in known as

A. cyberstalking.

B. a DDoS attack.

C. intimidation.

D. cyberterrorism.

11. The "right to erasure" involves people's right to

A. avoid meeting or being contacted by their biological parents when they themselves have been adopted.

B. have personal information related to them "erased" or removed from the internet.

C. restrict who sees their information on the internet.

D. avoid contact with ex-spouses, lovers, or partners.

12. Todd decides that a particular schoolmate is quite attractive, but she has told him that she is not interested in a relationship with him. He tracks down her home address and sends letters to her home, follows her around based on her Google Maps and Facebook check-in locations, and sends anonymous emails threatening her. Todd is guilty of

A. nothing, technically; none of those actions is illegal.

B. doxing.

C. assault and battery.

D. cyberstalking.

13. In 1990, a cancer patient named John Moore sued UCLA for using his cells and commercializing his cell line for research purposes. The California Supreme Court ruled that

A. UCLA was at fault, should have informed Moore, and owed Moore from the profits of the cell line.

B. UCLA was not at fault and was free to use Moore's cells however it chose, including the creation of a commercialized cell line.

C. fault was shared, but the university nonetheless owed Moore for his (unwitting) "contribution" to the "product" that was created.

D. Moore had signed away the rights to his cells and any subsequent cell cultures when he entered the hospital.

14. Autonomous vehicles create an interesting, problematic, and often ambiguous liability question, because

A. current law assumes that the person in the driver's seat is in control of the vehicle.

B. the vehicle could leave a driver stranded, with no way to take control of the vehicle.

C. current law assumes that the manufacturer is at fault, but in fact the passenger may have done something to disrupt the vehicle's software.

D. no one foresaw the development of such vehicles.

15. Computer professionals—by virtue of their claim to be professionals—have a number of professional and ethical obligations. Which of the following is NOT one of those obligations?

A. They have a presumed and unquestionable obligation of loyalty to their employers.

B. They have a presumed and unquestionable obligation to affirm the public good.

C. They have an unquestionable obligation to guard the privacy of customers' and users' data.

D. They have an obligation to provide full disclosure of all system capabilities, limitations, and potential problems.

16. People have always been able to lie, incite violence, and spread misinformation, but the advent of social media and the internet has given such people

A. the ability to couch their lies in more acceptable terms.
B. much more access and much greater visibility.
C. an excuse to incite hatred.
D. a reason to be angry at people with opposing viewpoints.

17. Researchers and ethicists studying the technology gap worry especially about students who encounter the gap. Why is that?

A. Given that students will, in a few years, be in positions of power, it is important that all students have computers.
B. A lack of technological literacy could exclude students from society by denying them technological literacy.
C. Students are young, and technology such as social media helps to form their social personalities.
D. Many older people do not understand technology very well; they need young people to learn about the technology so that they can then help older people master it.

18. As a result of what one ethicist has called its "logical malleability," the computer is essentially a "universal tool" that can perform many tasks—perhaps almost any task. Computers don't get tired, they need no sleep, they don't go home in the evening. As a result, computers have been seen as

A. the salvation of the middle class.
B. a threat to upper management.
C. a threat to workers.
D. a safety risk to workers.

19. Many technologies in the past have altered people's lives: the printing press, the automobile, the airplane, and many other technological advances. And yet, we do not have "printing press ethics" or "airplane ethics." Some ethicists have thus argued that

   A. computer professionals have no need to consider ethical issues.
   B. the focus of cyberethics ought to be limited to those issues that affect computer professionals.
   C. cyberethics as a term is useless, vague, ambiguous, and potentially harmful to the industry.
   D. computer professionals must embrace the study of the moral and social implications of the technologies with which they work.

20. Israeli-born Harvard Law School professor Yochai Benkler has studied the evolution of media, and believes that traditional media and the "new, networked media" have come together

   A. in a clash that will end with "the destruction of one or the other."
   B. in the form of "unpopular speech."
   C. to form a "new legal environment."
   D. in a "new media environment."

ANSWER KEY AND EXPLANATIONS

1. B	**5.** B	**9.** B	**13.** B	**17.** B
2. A	**6.** D	**10.** D	**14.** A	**18.** C
3. B	**7.** B	**11.** B	**15.** A	**19.** B
4. C	**8.** C	**12.** D	**16.** B	**20.** D

1. **The correct answer is B.** Net neutrality supporters argue that larger companies can afford the higher costs (or can pass those costs on to their customers), while smaller companies will be unable to absorb or pass on those costs; supporters say this would give large companies an advantage, thus stifling innovation. Providing tiered services would give large companies an advantage, thus eliminating choice A as a correct answer. Choices C and D reflect arguments *against* net neutrality.

2. **The correct answer is A.** Human error of one sort or another is ultimately responsible for the vast majority of network breaches. The other choices are all cybersecurity risks, but they do not rank as highly as human error; in fact, human error often leads to ransomware attacks, hackers breaching firewalls, and DDoS attacks.

3. **The correct answer is B.** The GDPR laws are quite strict and cover many aspects of privacy. Many in the United States feel that the laws are too restrictive compared to the laws that exist in the US. Complying with the GDPR laws is quite demanding and difficult.

4. **The correct answer is C.** In AR, the real world is enhanced by a computer, which often provides information about the subject. For instance, a smart phone app that overlays a camera view of a mountain with information about that mountain (name, size, location, etc.) would be an example of AR. A computer-generated world in which users live and interact (choice A) is called virtual reality, not augmented reality. A game that gamers can play online with thousands of others (choice B), is an MMORPG—a massively multiplayer online role-playing game. Pilots viewing readouts in mid-air is a common form of AR called heads-up display (HUD). However, while HUD is a form of AR, the more inclusive description provided in choice C is the best answer.

5. **The correct answer is B.** One tweet begets another, and candidates and staffers often end up retweeting false information. Choice A is incorrect because *all* candidates have access to the technology; if anything, the use of technology levels the playing field for candidates with less funds. Choice B is not true. The tweets are not "almost always" false and malicious, though we may or may not agree with their content. Choice D doesn't make sense. There's quite a lot of technology that did not exist in the world of the Founding Fathers, but that doesn't disallow or invalidate the use of the technology.

6. **The correct answer is D.** Intellectual property (IP) is property that includes rights to intangible creations—books, films, software, and designs, for example. Such property belongs to its creator(s), even though IP is not always something that can be seen, viewed, or touched. Real property (choice A) is real estate—immovable property, such as land and things (homes, etc.) that are attached to that land. Commercial property (choice B) is simply real property intended to generate a profit, while collective property (choice C) is property owned by a group of people.

7. **The correct answer is B.** Since computers in the 1940s and 1950s were not connected to one another (let alone to larger networks or to the internet), there was no easy way to access and steal data. Choice A is not true. One of the uses of the mainframes, for instance, was the collection and calculation of tax data; another was the tabulation of census data. Both of these can be construed as "personal" data. Choice C was not an issue because computer security was in its infancy at the time; there was very little to fear since mainframe computers were not connected to one another. Furthermore, it would be very difficult to access and steal data stored on such devices. Choice D was not an issue because the size of the computers (and they were very large, some of them room-sized or larger) had nothing to do with their security— other than the fact that it was unlikely that a person could enter a room and walk out with one.

8. **The correct answer is C.** In its announcement, Facebook never said it would report spammers and scammers to the authorities. There may be cases when the company would do that, but that was not part of the new program. All the other choices reflect statements made by Facebook when unveiling its new program.

9. **The correct answer is B.** A lawful access mandate allows law enforcement officers or intelligence agencies to seize and decrypt information, or to have companies decrypt it for them. Such a mandate does not protect data as choice A erroneously indicates; rather it gives law enforcement the ability to decrypt the data. The mandate would not require law enforcement agencies to request that the owner decrypt the data as choice C indicates; law enforcement may have already so requested, but the ruling would allow them to force decryption if necessary. Choice D is incorrect because the mandate would not specify or cause the destruction of the data.

10. **The correct answer is D.** Using the internet to threaten physical harm for ideological purposes is known as cyberterrorism. Deliberate disruption of computer systems and networks for those same purposes may also be deemed cyberterrorism. Cyberstalking (choice A) is the harassment of an individual via computer. A DDoS (distributed denial of service) attack (choice B) is a brute force attack on a server—it might or might not be connected to cyberterrorism. Intimidation (choice C) is a form of harassment, and would most likely be deemed cyberstalking.

11. **The correct answer is B.** Some countries have enacted laws that aim to protect people by allowing them to have personal information about themselves removed from the internet. The version of the GDPR adopted by the EU in 2016 guarantees the "right to erasure," though it specifies limits to that right. The "right to erasure" has nothing to do with adoption (choice A) or contact with ex-spouses and the like (choice D). It *does* have to do with who sees information (choice C), but not by restricting access to specific persons. Rather, it specifies that information can be completely removed—not that it can be viewed only by certain people.

12. **The correct answer is D.** Todd's actions amount to stalking via the—i.e., cyberstalking. He's threatening her and intimidating her, so he has stepped over the line into potentially illegal territory (thus negating choice A). Doxing (choice B) is the release of personal information, and Todd does not seem to have done that. If the schoolmate is intimidated by Todd's actions, that *could* constitute assault (choice C), but he has not made physical contact with her, so it could not be battery.

13. **The correct answer is B.** The Court determined that "a hospital patient's discarded blood and tissue samples are not his personal property, and that individuals do not have rights to a share in the profits earned from commercial products or research derived from their cells." Thus, UCLA was not at fault and was free to use Moore's cells as they so choose.

14. **The correct answer is A.** The law assumes that the person in the driver's seat is responsible for the actions of the vehicle, but in this case that may not be true. The vehicle could leave a driver stranded (choice B), but that has always been true. Current law does not assume that the manufacturer is at fault (choice C); it assumes that if anyone is at fault, it is a driver. It is not true that no one foresaw the development of autonomous vehicles (choice D); they have been a staple of science fiction for many years and a subject of serious research for almost as long.

15. **The correct answer is A.** Computer professionals *do* have a duty of loyalty to their employers, but it is not unquestionable. If it were unquestionable and absolute, that could conflict with the other principles. Perhaps the public good (choice B) would be best served by "blowing the whistle" on certain practices or issues, potentially including issues related to privacy (choice C) or system liabilities (choice D).

16. **The correct answer is B.** While the internet has democratized information, it has also democratized *mis*information. Anyone can "publish" on the internet, and its reach is enormous. People have always attempted to couch distasteful sentiments in terms that might be more acceptable to a larger number of people (choice A); social media did not give them that ability, though it widened their reach. Social media did not give people an excuse (choice C) to incite hatred or a reason to be angry (choice D). People have always had reasons and sought excuses; the internet may have made it easier to espouse such sentiments, but it did not give them a *reason* to do so.

17. **The correct answer is B.** Students are growing up in a technological world, and they're at an age where they learn to understand that world and gain knowledge about the news and about decisions being made that will affect them in the coming years. A lack of access to technology would exclude them from this new society by denying them key literacy skills and knowledge. There may be some truth to the other choices, but they do not represent specific concerns of social justice researchers.

18. **The correct answer is C.** Workers fear—sometimes rightly— that they can be replaced by computers (or by robots, which are essentially mobile computers that can interact with their environments). Since so many workers are members of the middle class (choice A), computers would hardly be seen as the "salvation" of that class. Nor would they pose much of a threat to upper management (choice B) or a safety risk to workers (choice D).

19. **The correct answer is B.** Some ethicists (Donald Gotterbarn, for one) have argued that computer scientists have no business considering broad moral questions unless they directly affect practitioners in their industry. These critics are not saying that professionals need not consider ethical issues at all (choice A), just that those considerations should be limited to issues relevant to the industry. No one is saying that the term is vague or ambiguous (choice C), merely that it's being applied too broadly. Gotterbarn and like-minded critics are saying the exact *opposite* of choice D; according to them, computer professionals should *not* consider the broader moral and social implications.

20. **The correct answer is D.** Benkler sees the two melding into a completely new, highly collaborative and networked thing. The two forces will not destroy one another (choice A), says Benkler, but will morph into a new form of media. The blending will not create or embody unpopular speech (choice B), but will require new laws to protect such speech. The new environment may require a reformed legal regime (choice C) that can account for the new players, but that is a side issue and not the result foreseen by Benkler.

DIAGNOSTIC TEST ASSESSMENT GRID

Now that you've completed the diagnostic test and read through the answer explanations, you can use your results to target your studying. Find the question numbers from the diagnostic test that you answered incorrectly and highlight or circle them below. Then focus extra attention on the sections within Chapter 3 dealing with those topics.

Ethics in Technology

Content Area	Topic	Question #
Cyberspace and Privacy	• Privacy and security in cyberspace • Individual conduct in cyberspace • Sharing with online communities and social networking services • Government surveillance • Corporate uses of personal data	2, 4, 8
Domestic and International Security	• Domestic and international regulations • Collection and use of personal data: national security • Hacking and counter-hacking • Information warfare • Cyberterrorism	3, 5, 7, 10
Legal Issues in Cyberspace	• Free speech issues • Privacy legislation and industry self-regulation • Intellectual property • Lawful access and encryption • Cybercrimes	6, 9, 11, 12
Technological Innovation and Ethics	• Biotechnologies • Internet of things • Robotics and artificial intelligence • Autonomous vehicles • Social justice issues	13, 14, 17, 18
Professional Ethics	• Moral obligations, legal liability, and accountability of corporations • Moral responsibilities of IT professionals • The role of the press • Social media: positive reinforcement and dissemination of unfounded information • Net neutrality	1, 15, 16, 19, 20

Chapter 3

Ethics in Technology Subject Review

OVERVIEW

- **Ethics, Ethicists, and Runaway Trolleys**
- **Cyberspace and Privacy**
- **Domestic and International Security**
- **Legal Issues in Cyberspace**
- **Technological Innovation and Ethics**
- **Professional Ethics**
- **New or Old? Created or Exacerbated?**
- **Summing It Up**

To explore a topic such as Ethics in Technology, you'll need to become familiar with some of the philosophical considerations that go into the study of ethics. You'll also need to become familiar with technology in general and with the specific applications of the technologies we use every day—computers, networks, social media, the internet, and so on. And don't forget the controversies associated with technology.

What we're talking about is known as **cyberethics**—the study of moral, legal, and social issues that are impacted by (in a few cases, some might say *caused by*) technology. Luckily, there's no need to get too buried in the minutiae of classical philosophical theories. And you won't be required to become a computer scientist. However, you will need a basic understanding of technologies and how ethical considerations are informed by these technologies.

ETHICS, ETHICISTS, AND RUNAWAY TROLLEYS

Let's begin our examination by looking at a couple of the basic terms and concepts you'll encounter in the study of ethics.

Those who study ethics fall into one of several schools of thought. One of these is **utilitarianism**, a "consequentialist" approach that tends to look at things from the perspective of a cost-benefit analysis; the consequences are what matter here. Often, this means that a question about whether something is moral or ethical seemingly comes down to a fairly straightforward equation: Does the action harm more people than it helps? Or does it help more people than it harms?

> **NOTE:** To learn more about utilitarianism, read about the lives of British philosopher Jeremy Bentham (1748–1832) and British philosopher/political economist John Stuart Mill (1806–1873).

To illustrate, let's consider the classic "runaway trolley" problem in which a trolley driver must determine which direction to head his out-of-control trolley. The answer seems fairly simple—at least, at first. The driver should turn in the direction (or in some versions, throw a switch that moves the trolley to a different track) that would result in the least loss of life; if the choice were between hitting a couple in one direction or a larger group in another, the driver would head for the couple because turning that direction would result in the fewest number of deaths or injuries.

> **NOTE:** The runaway trolley problem goes back at least to the early 1900s, when it was posed as part of a "railroad switchman's dilemma," and the person on the track was the switchman's child.

But ethical questions are rarely simple. For example, what if the couple on the corner are friends of the driver? What if the young "couple" was actually two young children, and the other group consisted of at-risk elderly persons out for a walk near their retirement center? Are the young children, with their lives yet ahead of them, "worth" more than the elderly, whom we may assume have already led full and productive lives? Ethical questions quickly become complex and value laden.

Another ethical paradigm, often seen as being at odds with utilitarianism, is **deontology**. Deontology is a "normative" ethical theory that says the morality of an action should be based not on its consequences, but on some "normative" ethical considerations based on duty, rules, or obligations. Here, the action itself is more important than the consequences. A deontologist in control of the trolley might decide to do *nothing*, because doing *something* would kill someone. Of course, doing nothing might also result in someone's death, and that is illustrative of one of the criticisms of deontology: what does one do when rights and duties conflict?

NOTE: To learn more about deontological approaches to ethics, read about German philosopher Immanuel Kant (1724–1804).

The "runaway trolley" dilemma might seem like an archaic example for a discussion of ethics in technology but consider for a moment the advent of autonomous vehicles. If you're "driving" along in your shiny new Tesla with the car itself in control, what happens when the vehicle is confronted with a choice analogous to that of the trolley driver? Let's say that a large couch has fallen off of a moving van just ahead of you and the car must suddenly swerve out of its lane in order to protect you. The vehicle's technological programming must "decide" which direction to swerve. The car's cameras "see" to the left a large group of schoolchildren on a field trip who are being led by a young teacher; to the right is a group of construction workers erecting scaffolding on a new building. One option, of course, is for the vehicle to slam on its brakes, but that could result in *you* being killed. Either way, someone is about to be injured or killed. Which direction should it go? What should the car "decide" to do? *Why* should it decide that?

In reality, the car itself doesn't make the decision. The decision has actually been made—perhaps many months ago—by a group of engineers and programmers. So now the moral dilemma has shifted from you to those engineers, and they are the ones who must weigh the ethical ramifications of their decisions. Perhaps unknowingly, the designers and programmers of autonomous vehicles have become ethicists.

Technology and ethics have—perhaps literally—collided, and out of the rubble of the wreckage emerges yet another interesting ethical question: Who should be accountable for the results of the "car's" decision? You? Tesla? The individual programmer? The driver of the vehicle that dropped the couch? We've reached the point where machines are making decisions, and because machines are supremely logical, we can be assured that an appropriately programmed machine (a vehicle, in this case) will make the "correct" decision. But, as Hewlett Packard Enterprise's Dr. Eng Lim Goh has noted, "What's correct may not always be right."

Again, there's nothing simple about the study of ethics, and this brief introduction doesn't even scratch the surface. Its purpose is simply to get you thinking about ethics and their consequences, and to see that technology does not free us from these sorts of considerations. If anything, technology tends to exacerbate and complicate ethical issues.

Let's take a look at some technologies that have affected ethical decision-making, and some of the ethical issues that have been created or exacerbated by these technologies. The DSST breaks down the areas of interest into five parts, so we'll do the same here. The areas are: Cyberspace and Privacy, Domestic and International Security, Legal Issues in Cyberspace, Technological Innovation and Ethics, and Professional Ethics.

CYBERSPACE AND PRIVACY

Privacy and Security in Cyberspace

Online, we're concerned with three types of security: network security, system security, and data security. There are certainly steps you can take to ensure that your home network and computing devices are secure— though much of that may be addressed by security applications and, at work, by a system administrator.

> **NOTE:** Did you know that the root cause of almost all security breaches is some form of human error? *People* are always the weak link in any system.

One of the most troubling security matters is the issue of data privacy. Knowingly and unknowingly, we share data all the time: We post information on social networks. We write passwords on sticky notes. We use laughably inept passwords like "password123" or "mypassword," so our accounts are hacked, and data is stolen. We are—often unknowingly—tracked by marketers, or by aggregators who collect information and sell it to marketers. Our browsing and buying habits are tracked across multiple websites, and that information is used to sell us products and predict (or even influence) our actions. The information we willingly or unwillingly share is known as **personally identifiable information (PII)**, which is data that can be used to trace our identities.

Of course, there are steps we can take to avoid oversharing our data. Various **privacy-enhancing tools (PETs)** protect against surveillance, masking our identities or making it impossible for watchers to determine the source of our searches and web page requests. Some of these tools work by obfuscation: browser add-ons like TrackMeNot create a flurry of false leads, creating a great deal of "noise" that makes it difficult to follow you. **Virtual Private Networks (VPNs)** create encrypted pipelines through which data can flow unmolested and unobserved.

Sometimes, though, we *want* to be tracked—to a point, at any rate. Websites use temporary **cookies** (also known as **session cookies**) to keep track of your visits and activities on that website. These first-party cookies are useful because they allow the site to know what you've seen on the various pages, and that you're the person with X items waiting in the site's online shopping cart. Session cookies are normally deleted when you exit the website, so the site's only "watching" you for a limited time.

> **NOTE:** You can delete cookies at any time by going to your browser's Settings menu. If you delete *all* cookies, you may find that you'll have to once again sign into websites that previously "remembered" who you were when you visited them.

Even **persistent first-party cookies**—ones that are *not* erased when you leave—can be helpful. After all, do you really *want* to have to sign in every time you access your favorite website? These cookies allow the site to remember you, take up very little space on your hard drive, and don't track you intrusively.

Third-party cookies—placed by someone other than the site you're visiting—can be useful, but they can also be used by advertiser networks that share your interest in whatever is discussed on that site with marketers. This is not always a terrible thing; the real issue is that your information and your interests are being shared with persons and companies you don't know, and that the information can then be sold to *other* marketing organizations, so that the data about you is no longer in your control.

One worrisome privacy development is **device fingerprinting**. Used in conjunction with cookies—sometimes **zombie cookies**, which reappear even after they've supposedly been deleted—this is technology that collects information about a specific device for the purpose of identifying the device and its user. Device fingerprinting can be used to help prevent identity theft, but it can also be used to compile long-term browsing histories and track your behavior across multiple websites. Again, you've lost control of information that belongs to you and is, in fact, *about* you.

Sometimes your machines betray you. For example, a **Machine Identification Code (MIC)** is a digital watermark included on every laser printout to identify the specific printer—not the brand or model, but the exact printer—used to create that printout. The technology was created to help track down counterfeiters, but it's another example of information about you (in this case, about whatever you're printing) that is not in your control.

When you *do* lose control of your information, one result can be **identity theft**. Criminals can use information gleaned about you—or taken in a breach from another party, such as the 2017 Equifax breach, in which almost 150 million social security numbers and 200 million credit card numbers were exposed—to establish credit in your name or to obtain some other financial gain. Many times, hackers will simply gather identities and then sell them to persons seeking access to another identity. (Some sources estimate that about $20 is the going price for a stolen identity.)

One interesting take on the loss of privacy is Helen Nissenbaum's analysis of what she calls the issue of **contextual integrity**. Nissenbaum, a professor at Cornell Tech, points out that we're comfortable sharing data when we can select—and control—the context. That is, we're willing to share private information in one context, based on our trust that the information will not be shared in some other context. For instance, you may be happy to share your disease symptoms with your doctor, but not at all happy to discover that she has shared them with an insurance or pharmaceutical company, or with her spouse or tennis partner.

NOTE: Dr. Helen Nissenbaum is a professor of information science at Cornell Tech. She is the editor, with Deborah G. Johnson, of *Computers, Ethics & Social Values*.

In all of these scenarios, your information and information about you is no longer in your control. And that's the primary ethical issue about data privacy: **data sovereignty**. Who owns that data? Who has control over it? And if you agree to share it with one group, does that mean that the group can share it with (i.e., sell it to) another group? In addition to the fact that someone can use information about you to either attack you or sell you something, the root argument is one of ownership—it's your information and, say most ethicists, you should be the one to decide what happens with it.

Individual Conduct in Cyberspace

We tend to describe cyberethics issues as things that arise when "they" do something—groups of people, the government, marketers, hackers, etc. But really, much of the problem comes down to individual conduct. People are individuals, and they can behave well or badly, depending on the circumstances. Unfortunately, the internet provides a shield of anonymity, or at least of distance, behind which some people do or say things that they would not do or say in face-to-face situations.

Sometimes this involves the misuse (or fear of misuse) of an otherwise promising technology. The first iteration of Google Glass was an interesting and potentially beneficial use of **augmented reality (AR)** technology in which information about what the wearer was seeing was overlaid on a tiny screen. One of the features of Glass, though, was that it included video-recording capabilities. This worried people, as it was not always possible to know when you were being recorded. (The first version of Google Glass was a flop, largely for this reason.)

> **NOTE:** In May 2019, Google released the Google Glass Enterprise Edition 2, an Android-based system with a faster processor and a screen that only powers on when the system senses that you're looking at it.

Sometimes online confrontations erupt into online hate messaging, and sometimes they go even further, escalating into doxing or swatting. **Doxing** (or *doxxing*) is collecting and publishing someone's personal information (or "docs"), which can lead to real-life stalking or can affect someone's work or personal life. **Swatting** is potentially even worse. In a swatting attack, an attacker will phone a fake bomb report (or other serious issue requiring a police presence) using the address of a target—who may not know he or she is the subject of an attack. The goal is to get the police (perhaps even a SWAT team) to show up—armed, nervous, and ready to force entry to the target's home or office. Obviously, this is a potentially tragic situation, and swatting has resulted in at least one death.

> **NOTE:** In 2019, Californian Tyler Barriss was sentenced to 20 years in prison after he "swatted" Andrew Finch, a resident of Wichita, Kansas. The call ended in Finch's death when he dropped his hands after police had told him to raise them. Barriss had a record of making fake calls.

One example of online attacks that got way out of hand is **gamergate**, a harassment campaign by various (mostly male) gamers who attacked a (mostly female) group of gamers and developers, doxing and swatting them and forcing some to abandon their homes and jobs. Given the potentially lethal results of swatting, one gamergate principal, Zoe Quinn, called swatting "a form of attempted murder."

We've all seen movies in which hackers sitting in a basement burrow through a firewall, cracking passwords left and right, until they arrive at the information they want. That does happen, but it's fairly rare, because there's a much easier way for a criminal to get information: just *ask* for it, or, alternatively, trick someone into giving it up. This type of "hacking" is called **social engineering**, a form of attack that relies mainly on deceit and trickery. Sending someone a fake email (or a doctored link in an email), an approach called **phishing**, is a form of social engineering. So is something as low-tech as having someone show up at an office wearing a work shirt and cap with a company logo and then wandering around the building looking for passwords on sticky notes while he or she "services" your printer or HVAC system.

Another form of social engineering, one that's common on dating or romance sites (but which also shows up on sites such as Facebook and others) is called **catfishing**. This is the creation of a fake profile (often displaying someone of a different gender than the actual gender of the attacker) in an attempt to get money by requesting "help" with medical expenses, airfare (sometimes supposedly needed to allow the person to come visit the target), etc. Many people looking for romance—or simply for friendship—are "catfished" every year.

The essential ethical issue here is that people sometimes behave badly when they believe they cannot be brought to account for their behavior—and the internet encourages that behavior by providing a shield behind which troublemakers can hide. Psychologists call this effect **disinhibition**, noting that hiding behind the anonymity of the internet greatly reduces the fear that would ordinarily inhibit us from acting in this fashion.

NOTE: Disinhibition does not just occur online. Psychologists define it as a lack of restraint and disregard of social conventions, whatever the cause or context.

Sharing with Online Communities and Social Networks

In spite of the disinhibition effect, most users (and social network providers) feel that online anonymity is an important feature. Yes, it's easier to act in an unethical manner when you're either anonymous or hiding behind a fictitious persona, but there are some people (dissidents, protesters, whistleblowers, journalists) who need that anonymity in order to stay safe. This presents us with another ethical dilemma, of course: There are probably more people hurt by anonymity (in the form of faceless harassment and attacks) than helped by it. If we take the consequentialist, utilitarian ethical approach, we would consider that the many people who are harmed by anonymous attacks outweigh the few who benefit from the anonymity. On the other hand, an ethicist from the normative school—a deontologist—would say that what matters is what is the *right* thing to do, regardless of the numbers. (Keep in mind that we're deliberately taking a somewhat simplistic approach. There are many other schools of ethical thought, some of which aim to resolve quandaries such as this.)

As has often been said, "words matter." Whether it's the disinhibition effect or something else, people get angry on social media, and they lash out. Sometimes the lashing out crosses boundaries and becomes hate speech, instances of which have increased dramatically over the past several years. In extreme cases, online confrontations have resulted in physical attacks on people, resulting in injuries or death. For example, there have been Facebook posts by attackers who ultimately killed or injured people. In most cases, the posts remained up until after the attacks. In cases like that, who is responsible? Obviously, the person who carried out the attack is responsible—but does the platform bear some responsibility for not having policed itself or reacted in a timely fashion? As we'll see later, social networking platforms in the US are generally *not* held liable for the content or actions of those posting on the platform. Section 230 of the 1996 Communications Decency Act specifically shields platform providers from such liability. But liability and *responsibility* are two different things: one is a legal term, the other has more to do with morality and ethics.

Facebook, by far the largest and most influential social networking platform, has made sporadic attempts to deal with the ethical issues posed by the hoaxes, fake news, and hate speech that have appeared on its site. Recently, the social media giant unveiled a program designed to address the problem. The program includes working with third-party fact checkers (including FactCheck.org, PolitiFact, and the Associated Press) and allowing users to flag posts as "disputed" or to indicate in some other way that a post is a hoax or of dubious origin.

The thing to keep in mind about all of this is that the purpose of Facebook, Twitter, and the like is *not* to further communication or to connect groups of people: the real purpose of Facebook is to make money. These sites are businesses, and they make money by allowing paid ("sponsored") posts and by collecting data and selling it to marketers (who sometimes turn around and resell it to other marketers). We would like to think that, given the choice, Facebook and the others would make ethical choices, but much of the time their decisions will be based not on ethics but on profit. Moves that might negatively affect their revenue tend to be unpopular with the company's executives and shareholders.

We can disagree over the motivations of social networking sites, but there's no denying that they're incredibly popular. People love to meet (or catch up with) other people, they enjoy making their opinions known, and they like sharing their lives with others. However, people tend to share those portions of their lives that are, or can be presented as, positive, healthy, and happy. When we view others' posts and profiles, we're often not seeing what their lives are really like. This causes some problems that we'll discuss momentarily.

Much of what we see on social media and other sites is what is termed **clickbait**: links that serve the purpose of getting one to click on the link, even if the target of that link is content that turns out to be of dubious interest. Its purpose is not to inform, but to take advantage of your curiosity so that you'll click, thus raising the number of views the site can claim.

> **NOTE:** If a click takes the user to a slideshow (a series of images, each on its own page), each one of *those* clicks can also be used to inflate the site's numbers.

Sometimes what we're viewing (and liking and sharing) isn't real content at all—or isn't posted by whom you think posted it. Facebook, for example, said that in the run-up to the 2016 US election, roughly 29 million people read content in their feeds that originated from Russian-based bots and trolls. A Russian "PR" agency had posted roughly 80,000 times over a two-year period. (Some disinformation attempts, though effective, are not particularly sophisticated, and their agents not particularly smart; the Russian posts were uncovered, in the end, because so many of the paid posts were paid for in rubles.)

Still, social media is immensely popular, and one of the reasons is that *it makes us feel good*—literally. When we hear our computer, phone, or tablet chime, that's a form of positive reinforcement. Even if it's not necessarily good news, it's still news and still evidence that someone has attempted to make a connection with us. We like that. We like it so much that psychologists have termed it a form of addiction; we eventually get to the point where we *need* that almost-constant positive reinforcement. Those connections make us feel more connected and thus more in control of our lives.

One of the problems with this is that we end up constantly comparing our lives to others, and often this feeds our insecurities. Although the contact makes us feel good, the overall effect can lower our self-esteem over time, because we're constantly comparing ourselves to people who seemingly have perfect lives, clean homes, well-behaved children, exciting jobs, and fabulous vacations. The ironic result is that heavy users of social media can end up feeling more socially isolated, in spite of the enormous amount of time that we spend "socializing" on Facebook or Twitter or Snapchat. (And social isolation has been associated with serious health problems, among other issues.)

In the end, we collect Facebook friends (and "likes" and "shares") almost as if it were a contest. Yet, more people are reporting that in spite of all of this digital connectivity, they actually have fewer close confidants than in years before. Much of the time, these social media contacts are not real friends, and, in the long term, our addiction to the social media networks may be doing us more harm than good.

There's another problem with social media—or more specifically, with the algorithms that determine what we see in our feeds. As you "like" or respond to certain type of content from certain types of people, you see more of that type of content. In a way, this is a good thing—who doesn't want to hear from or about like-minded people? But taken to an extreme, it can mean that we're exposed to more and more opinions with which we already agree, while we're simultaneously exposed to fewer and fewer opinions and information with which we disagree. The result is what has been called a **social media bubble** or an **echo chamber** in which we hear only echoes of ourselves (or of people who agree with us) and little or nothing from those with whom we might disagree. This might be pleasant, but there's a great disadvantage to not exposing ourselves to alternative viewpoints: Those who believe in a certain way simply hear from others who believe similarly, and we continually rail away at opposing viewpoints without ever having really being exposed to them. This is exceedingly polarizing and, as some ethicists have noted, may threaten what we think of as "deliberative democracy." After all, how can one be deliberate if one does not see both sides of an issue?

Cyberspace and Privacy—Government Surveillance

In addition to sharing (or possibly oversharing) on social media sites and as a result of social engineering attacks, we have yet another privacy issue with which to contend: government surveillance. Government agencies (local, regional, and federal) collect data about us for a variety of reasons. Supporters argue that the government needs to collect information, and that we need to give up some privacy in exchange for more security. While few would argue with the need for information when tracking down terrorists or other criminals, how that data is acquired (and what happens to it afterward) has led to some sticky ethical questions.

For example, **PRISM** is a once-secret government surveillance program under which the US government collects communications from various internet companies. The government argues that the program targets only foreigners, but some groups, including the ACLU, have accused the government of spying on US citizens. When National Security Agency (NSA) contractor Edward Snowden leaked details of the program in 2013, a huge debate erupted over whether Snowden had broken the law by sharing secret government documents. Then another debate erupted over whether there might be some circumstances in which he was justified, or even *obligated*, to break the law in order to serve a greater good.

> **NOTE:** The PRISM program is still active. It was renewed in 2018 with no meaningful opposition.

Another program exposed by the Snowden documents was **MYSTIC**, an NSA program that could record the complete contents of all phone calls in an entire country. That's a great deal of data, but the NSA has built its Utah Data Center, a data storage facility capable of storing exabytes of data, so it's not out of the question from a technological perspective. Snowden also exposed the NSA's Bullrun program, which was aimed at cracking the encryption of online communications. Snowden stole and then released (through Julian Assange's WikiLeaks and other outlets) thousands of secret NSA documents, and then took refuge in Moscow, which offered him temporary asylum.

The NSA *is* allowed to spy on citizens in certain circumstances. As part of the 2001 Patriot Act expansion of **FISA** (the 1978 Foreign Intelligence

Surveillance Act), NSA authorities were allowed to conduct surveillance on US citizens who were communicating with citizens or residents of foreign countries. The intelligence agency says that such data-gathering is necessary in the face of the growing number of terrorist attacks.

While the NSA is behind many of the data collection efforts that worry some citizens, it's not the only agency that has been accused of overreach. For example, the FBI's **Carnivore** program, which required physical installation at an internet service provider (ISP), monitored email, and other electronic communications. Local and state law enforcement agencies across Canada, the US, and the UK have used Harris Corporation's **Stingray**, a device that can mimic a cell tower, forcing all communications to flow through the device, where they can be intercepted. The privacy issue associated with such a device is that it captures *all* cellular traffic in the area, not just calls to and from those who are suspected of crimes.

NOTE: The NSA's mandate is technically restricted to spying on foreign countries by gathering intelligence via such tools as its Computer Network Operations group. The agency is forbidden by that mandate from spying on a US citizen, unless that citizen is an agent of a foreign power.

The debate rages on, and we are presented with an ethical conundrum: Are there times when a whistleblower such as Snowden is *obligated* to blow that whistle? Might he do irreparable harm to government efforts to combat terrorism? Or does he do more harm by allowing the government to snoop on citizens? Is Snowden a traitor? Are all whistleblowers traitors? If so, are there times when the country *needs* traitors? Is it permissible to capture innocent civilians' conversations in a Stingray digital dragnet, along with those of suspects?

Similarly, we have encountered ethical issues regarding **dark phones**—those that are protected or otherwise secured. Some argue that law enforcement agencies need access to the information in such devices, while others insist that cracking that encryption would be an invasion of privacy.

It's not only government agencies that have been accused of spying on citizens. In February 2017, the German government banned the sale of the My Friend Cayla doll, a children's toy that uses Bluetooth to transmit audio recordings, which were then stored by the manufacturer on a server owned by Nuance communications. The government banned the sale of the doll after it was discovered that Nuance sold voice data to the military and defense industries. Data, as we have said before, has value; in the aggregate, it has *enormous* value, and both governments and private companies will seek to benefit from it.

Again, the main issue here is privacy—who owns the data about you or that you have in your possession? It's an ethical problem that, as with most ethical problems, does not admit to a simple solution. Law enforcement agencies *do* need information in order to do their jobs, which is to protect us. Citizens *do* require and deserve privacy. Our ethical dilemma resides at the place where those two needs come into conflict.

In the United States, we live in a democracy, and we are both protected by and protected *from* our government. Are there times when a government agency must act in an undemocratic manner in order to protect the very democracy it serves? That's the root of the ethical argument about data privacy and government access to that data: Should we be prepared to give up some privacy in exchange for greater security? How much privacy are we prepared to cede in exchange for what level of security?

Corporate Uses of Personal Data

The final issue in our quick look at data privacy has to do not with governments seeking your data, but with corporations and what they do with the data they collect from and about you.

Not surprisingly, there's an immense amount of data out there, and companies want to collect as much of it as possible and use it to further their business interests. Hence the term **big data**, a phrase that refers not only to the size of the data collection efforts (massive), but also to the data's structure—or lack of structure. Data in a database is organized in such a way that parts of one record can easily be related to another, and records in one database can easily be tied to similarly structured information in another database. But big data collects huge amounts of possibly unrelated and unstructured data (generally, datasets that are too large or complex to be processed by traditional means), and then uses massive computing power (and sometimes artificial intelligence) to make sense of that information. It takes a great deal of computational muscle, more than a little time, and a fair amount of money to mine big data. Companies examine the data, looking for patterns that they can use to predict behavior and trends. Other companies, such as **data brokers**, may aggregate the data. analyze it, and sell the results of their analysis.

It's important to keep in mind that not all data mining is detrimental to the public's well-being. Data mining can be used to help discover human rights violations, analyze long-term weather patterns, or examine information from a huge network of sensors in order to monitor air pollution, among many other positive uses.

Sometimes companies wish to collect data about you so that they can determine whether you're a good investment; credit card companies, credit reporting agencies, and insurance companies know that the more information about you they can gather, the more accurate (and profitable) of an assessment they can make. This is why credit reporting agencies look for such things as phone call and texting data (including the duration of calls and frequently called numbers), address stability, and club and subscription activity. Their research has shown that people who make certain types of calls, take part in certain kinds of activities, and live at one address for long periods of time are good investments; their data-mining efforts are often aimed at analyzing this information to determine whether you are a good risk.

As we've seen, data mining isn't all bad, but one ethical issue resulting from the collection and analysis of such data has to do with agency, a term that we'll encounter several times in this summary. We're used to having **agency**—that is, the ability to make decisions about things that affect us: what to buy, where to go, whom to associate with, whom to vote for, etc. When businesses mine big data looking for patterns, associations, and trends, one of the things they sometimes wish to do is influence us, affecting our political beliefs, buying habits, and more. When they do that, we lose agency—we're not only no longer in complete control of our actions, but we don't even *know* that we're not in control of our actions. When we lose some measure of control over our behavior—especially when that loss occurs without our knowledge—then we have lost agency, our capacity to make decisions about our lives and even our beliefs.

Data mining operations and the accumulation and analysis of that much data—and the uses companies might make of it—do bring up ethical issues, but even small-scale corporate data collection can bring up ethical concerns.

Take, for example, the sharing of your web activities among multiple marketing organizations. It's fairly obvious that marketers associated with a specific site can (and, understandably, do) make note of where you're going on their sites, what you purchase, and the products and services in which you show an interest. But you may not realize that marketers associated with certain sites collect and then share (sell) that data. This is why, when you look at hiking boots on a website, you may start seeing ads for hiking boots—and other camping and backpacking gear—on other sites you visit; your interest in hiking boots has been noted and shared with "marketing partners" who pay to get data from the original site on which you viewed the hiking boots. Many websites, though not all, partner with marketing groups to collect and share that data with the various partners. And sometimes those partners sell that data to *other* partners.

This is a good example of both a loss of agency and an erosion of what Helen Nissenbaum called contextual integrity. The information that you were willing to share with a website called Larry's Boots and Such has now been passed on. It may be used to sell you boots, or perhaps to sell you items *related* to boots: tents, socks, backpacks, leather conditioner, camp stoves, etc. Two things have happened: You've lost control of the data, and therefore your agency has been diminished. Perhaps more importantly in this example, the contextual integrity of the information has been violated; you were willing to share with Larry's Boots and Such, but *not* willing to share with other companies, especially companies you've never heard of and with whom you did not know you were sharing. It happens all the time, though; your visit to a website can trigger a variety of hidden data-sharing mechanisms distributed across several companies.

NOTE: Interested in seeing which sites share data with which marketing groups? There are privacy enhancing tools (PETs) that you can install as an add-on to your web browser that can tell you with whom your favorite website is sharing data with.

Is this type of sharing ethical? Is it appropriate for someone to collect information about you and then share it without your knowledge? Perhaps not—although you may have consented to exactly that when you agreed to the site's terms and conditions. (Did you actually read those? Probably not; they're very long, complicated documents written in legalese—few people read them.)

But it gets worse.

Device fingerprinting is a relatively new development. This is a technique for linking a specific device (computer, phone, etc.) to a specific person— you. Once that has been done, it's easy to track you across websites so that the advertiser can see what sorts of sites you visit, the subjects in which you appear to be interested, and similar information. Note that the advertiser has not necessarily identified you personally; the advertiser only knows that a particular person who generally uses the device tends to visit specific sites. This type of tracking is occurring in real time, generally for the benefit of different marketing organizations.

Most of the data we've talked about here is anonymized. Generally, it's collected and then aggregated with other users' data—none of whom are specifically identified—and then the collected data is used to identify trends or market certain types of products to certain types of people. However, experiments have shown that it's possible to cross-reference anonymous data with other data in order to *re-identify* the original data sources. Experimenters did just this with a sample of supposedly anonymous Netflix data in 2006. Similarly, Belgian researchers analyzing 1.5 million cellphone users found that just four points of reference was enough to uniquely identify 95 percent of them. When this occurs, the user's data *and* anonymity is compromised.

Privacy groups and government organizations are aware of the issue. Most browsers implemented **Do Not Track (DNT)** requests in the mid-2000s, but these are voluntary; companies are free to ignore such requests, and most do, including (ironically, perhaps) Microsoft and Google. There are laws meant to safeguard your online privacy, and they will be discussed further. In the meantime, setting your browser to include DNT requests may not do much good; the browser may do so, but the sites you visit will probably ignore those requests.

DOMESTIC AND INTERNATIONAL SECURITY

Domestic and International Regulations

Many laws have been passed—both in the United States and internationally—in attempts to protect both domestic and international security, as well as privacy. Many of the acts aimed at safeguarding security are better known by their acronyms than by their actual names. We'll provide both here.

Two US acts that have domestic security and privacy as goals are the **Family Educational Rights and Privacy Act (FERPA)**, which describes who can have access to what sorts of student information, and the **Health Insurance Portability and Accountability Act (HIPAA)**, which protects health data from being overshared.

In an attempt to keep up with changing technology, the **Health Information Technology for Economic and Clinical Health Act (HITECH Act)** was passed in 2009. The act is meant to expand the role of health information technology while ensuring that health information remains secure. The HITECH Act does not supersede HIPAA but is intended to complement the earlier act by requiring entities covered by HIPAA to report data breaches that affect 500 or more persons to the US Department of Health and Human Services, to the media, and to the people affected by the breaches.

Companies and other entities that process or manage credit card transactions are entrusted with a great deal of important confidential data. Because of that, the **Payment Card Industry Data Security Standard (PCI-DSS)** regulates how that data must be handled. Any company or entity that handles credit card transactions must comply with the PCI-DSS requirements.

Data breaches of one sort or another have been a problem ever since there was data to breach. In the computer age, the issue has mushroomed, and now every state (plus Puerto Rico, the District of Columbia, and the US Virgin Islands) requires some sort of notification to affected customers or clients if their data is exposed. Note that this reporting is due to an array of state statutes, not federal law; there is no unified federal law under which breach reporting is required.

> **NOTE:** Any merchant who processes, stores, or transmits credit card data is required to be PCI compliant. If your business accepts credit cards but you do not wish to deal with PCI-DSS requirements, then you have the option of dealing with (and paying for) a third-party processing vendor that *is* subject to PCI-DSS. In that case, you simply read in—but do not store—a small piece of credit card information; that data is passed on to the vendor, who then completes the transaction and sends you back an "OK" or a "denied" signal.

Other acts and agencies, domestic and international, have security as their focus, rather than privacy. These days, when terrorist attacks of all sorts and international crime (often abetted by technology) have become epidemic, the laws and the methods of the agencies empowered to enforce them raise ethical questions to which there are no simple answers: How much security is enough? How much power should these agencies have? Have some laws granted agencies too much power while neglecting to provide appropriate oversight? Or must concerns about personal privacy give way to domestic and international security issues?

In the United States, the **Department of Homeland Security (DHS)** is a cabinet-level umbrella department that oversees a massive collection of agencies: The Transportation Security Administration, the US Coast Guard, the Federal Emergency Management Agency, US Immigration and Customs Enforcement, the United States Secret Service, and many other agencies are all components of the DHS. The department commands an aggregate budget of about $40 billion and has about 240,000 employees.

Among many other acts, the DHS now controls—through its sub-agencies—many aspects of immigration through the 1952 **Immigration and Nationality Act**, which governs the admission (and removal) of aliens and grants of asylum.

In 2002, the **Federal Information Security Management Act (FISMA)** came into effect, requiring all federal agencies—including the DHS and its sub-agencies—to develop methods of protecting their information systems.

As a measure of its concern over unchecked—and potentially unverified—immigration into the United States, the DHS administers a program called E-Verify. **E-Verify** is a voluntary program that allows employers to confirm the eligibility of potential employees. Note that the program is mandatory in the case of contracted federal workers and vendors.

Another proposed program that would be administered by the DHS through the **Cybersecurity and Infrastructure Security Agency (CISA)** is the **Ammonium Nitrate Security Program (ANSP)**. Ammonium nitrate is a component of some forms of fertilizer, but it can also be—and has been—used to create explosives that can be used in a terrorist attack. The chemical was used in 1995 by Timothy McVeigh to attack a federal building in Oklahoma City.

After the September 11, 2001, attacks, a number of laws were passed with the intent of protecting the country and its citizens from terrorist attacks. The **Critical Infrastructure Information Act (CIIA),** passed in 2002, was intended to require the sharing of information felt to be vital to the protection of the country. It required that infrastructure providers (those whose companies or agencies provide gas, electric, water, and other such utilities) communicate with government personnel as a way to reduce the country's vulnerability to terrorism.

Also following the September 11, 2001 attacks, agencies scrambled to figure out who was involved and what could be done to head off subsequent attacks. One of the results of that scramble was the discovery that the agencies often had no efficient way to share information—most of them operated in "silos" in which information that might have been useful to other agencies was never shared. One result of that discovery was that parts of the PATRIOT Act were aimed at tearing down those silos. Section 203 of the PATRIOT Act empowers law enforcement officials to share criminal investigative information that contains foreign intelligence or counterintelligence with intelligence and national-security personnel. Section 905 of the act requires that the attorney general disclose to the CIA any foreign intelligence acquired by the Department of Justice in the course of a criminal investigation.

The result of the sharing of this data may well be that we are safer from terrorist attack, but it does exacerbate the issue of data privacy, again bringing up the question of how much privacy we must agree to relinquish in exchange for improved security. After all, humans are making these decisions—determining what constitutes information worthy of being shared, and with whom it should be shared. Humans make mistakes or are influenced unduly by ideology; ethicists and privacy experts worry that, in their zeal to protect the citizenry, some agencies may overstep their bounds, or that shared data might end up being *overshared* data.

Note that international cooperation in response to terrorist attacks has sometimes been spotty, as some countries are reluctant to share important information or work too closely with others. After the spring 2019 terrorist attacks in Christchurch, New Zealand, the country's prime minister circulated a pledge aimed at eliminating terrorist and violent extremist content online as a way of preventing the internet from being used as a tool by terrorists. Many governments and several tech companies agreed to the commitments outlined and pledged to collaborate to help meet those commitments. Companies that signed the pledge include Google, Facebook, and Microsoft. France, Australia, Germany, India, and Sweden all signed the pledge, though the United States, Saudi Arabia, Mexico, and many other countries did not.

Collection and Use of Personal Data: National Security

Generally speaking, US intelligence and law enforcement agencies are not supposed to collect data about citizens unless they are suspected of a crime, but in 2013 it was alleged by NSA contractor Edward Snowden that the agency had collected private information about American citizens who were not under suspicion of any crimes. Snowden "blew the whistle" on the agency, releasing thousands of classified documents through WikiLeaks and other media outlets. The US Department of Justice accused Snowden of violating the Espionage Act of 1917, as well as theft of government property, which set off a debate that still rages.

Ethicists have set up frameworks within which **whistleblowing** can be considered and the whistleblower's behavior ranked on a scale that attempts to determine whether the release of information was justified—or perhaps even obligatory. There are, say most ethicists, times that an employee's obligation (or a citizen's) can conflict with other moral obligations.

For example, University of Kansas professor and business ethicist Richard T. De George (about whom you will learn more later) has created a framework designed to determine when an employee is *permitted* to "blow the whistle" on a practice or policy, and when the employee is *obligated* to do so. According to the framework, the employee is permitted (but not yet obligated) to blow the whistle if (1) the policy will do "serious and considerable harm" to the public, (2) the employee(s) have reported the "serious threat" to their immediate supervisor and have made "their moral concern known," and (3) the employee(s) have exhausted the "internal procedures and possibilities" within the organization, including going to the board of directors, if necessary.

On the other hand, the employee (says De George) is *obligated* to blow the whistle if the previous three criteria *and* two more have been met: (4) The employee(s) have "accessible, documented evidence that would convince a reasonable, impartial observer that one's view of the situation is correct," and (5) The employee(s) have "good reasons to believe that by going public the necessary changes will be brought about."

We can (and many of us no doubt will) argue about Snowden's actions, but De George's framework at least gives us a rational and somewhat objective starting point for that argument. Other ethicists have taken issue with De George's framework, and several other frameworks or criteria have been proposed. For our purposes here, it's enough to know that ethicists have discussed the issue of whistleblowing and devoted a great deal of thought to whether the role of whistleblower is a moral one, and if whistleblowing is or is not permitted under various circumstances. From the ethicists' perspective, a whistleblower is not inevitably to be condemned, but neither is the individual automatically viewed as a heroic figure.

Recall that in the early days of computers, data security wasn't much of an issue because computers were not connected to one another? Well, a lot has changed since then. Computers can not only be connected to each other but also via the internet to a vast array of networks. With the advent of **cloud storage**—data residing on collections of servers that may be located anywhere in the world—many computers don't store data locally anymore.

> **NOTE:** By definition, the "cloud" you're using may consist of multiple servers, each of which may store some piece of your data and which are linked together and which each contribute packets of data when you opt to view that data. Often, your cloud storage data is not only on one server, but on multiple servers located in multiple places around the world, depending on where your cloud provider can get the best prices for storage.

Cloud storage is all well and good, but—you may not be surprised to hear this—there can be security problems associated with saving your data on someone's server or on collections of servers. Several celebrities and others discovered this in 2014 when hackers breached Apple Corporation's iCloud cloud storage service where they stole and distributed nude photos, many of them belonging to celebrities, including model Kate Upton and actress Jennifer Lawrence. In some cases, the celebrities had actually erased the photos and had assumed that they were therefore safe from prying eyes; they were wrong, because although they had erased their *local* copies of those images, the cloud copies remained on Apple's supposedly secure iCloud storage servers.

The plundering of nude images of Jennifer Lawrence or Kate Upton is not, one assumes, a matter of national security. The issue is, however, much bigger than that. Some two billion people worldwide use cloud storage in some form. Their data is not in their hands and may be at risk of being hacked—either by criminals or by the agencies of one government or another.

Sometimes, it's our own government that seeks access to our data. There has been an increase lately in the number of demands made by the US government for data, often in the name of national security, and studies have concluded that existing legal frameworks in most countries (not just the United States) provide an inadequate foundation to allow systematic access while also protecting citizens' privacy (and other) rights.

Sporadic attempts have been made to codify and regulate the processing of personal data in the United States. In fact, the **Consumer Privacy Bill of**

Rights, proposed during the Obama era, requested that Congress grant the Federal Trade Commission (FTC) the ability to enforce the bill's provisions. The "bill" is really a collection of legislative attempts to regulate the processing of electronic personal data. The bill has not come to fruition, though it has evolved into several similar or related proposals. In 2020, consumer data privacy legislation is being considered in at least 30 states and in Puerto Rico, but very few bills have been enacted due to the global pandemic.

In the meantime, it's difficult to protect personal data, especially if it resides in the cloud where others can get at it. The **Clarifying Lawful Overseas Use of Data (CLOUD) Act** of 2018 amends the **Stored Communications Act (SCA)**, which is a part of the **Electronic Communications Privacy Act** of 1986, by allowing federal authorities to compel US tech companies to provide subpoenaed data stored on US or foreign servers. Most of these requests are made in the name of national security or drug trafficking enforcement.

Earlier we looked at the issue of corporate data collection, noting that when companies collect our information, we lose both agency and contextual integrity. That's potentially problematic, but some ethicists contend that government data collection is potentially much worse, because the government can restrict your liberty based on the data it collects. Companies might collect a great deal of data about you, but corporations can't take actions that restrict your liberties; the government, on the other hand, can prosecute and even jail you.

Still, some say that the most egregious data collections are performed by private corporations. In 2015, Senator Sheldon Whitehouse (D, Rhode Island) wrote an opinion piece in which he made that point, noting that, while we often complain about government data-collection, we seem to have no problem allowing corporations access to more and more private information. Whitehouse attributes much of the problem to the tension between personal privacy and national security.

Sometimes it's difficult to draw the line between personal and corporate or business data. In 2016, hackers believed to be under Russian control hacked and released the Democratic National Committee's emails, which were subsequently published by DCLeaks and then WikiLeaks. The collection of data included over 19,000 emails and over 8,000 attachments. (Hackers also penetrated GOP organizations, but gathered only older emails, according to then-FBI director James Comey.)

When governments collect personal data in the name of national security, we can't always be sure of the legality or the effectiveness of those programs. A 2013 independent White House report concluded that it could find no evidence that any terrorist attacks were stopped because of the NSA's data collection. This was in spite of President Obama previously having stated that least 50 threats had been averted because of this information. In the meantime, since surveillance efforts began ramping up with the "war on terror" declaration in 2001, the number of terrorist attacks has increased.

The United States is far from the only government wishing to access private data, sometimes for good reason. (And other governments are often *much* more heavy-handed about acquiring such information.) Ethicists worry, though, about opening the floodgates, about allowing governments (whatever the government being discussed) to access the private data of their citizens. Most would agree that the war on terror is a good cause, but it's difficult to guarantee that citizens' erosion of both agency and contextual integrity will stop there.

One thing that doesn't seem to be in dispute is the idea that foreign agents have attempted to influence elections around the world via the acquisition of private data and the posting of misinformation on various social networking sites. In 2017, for instance, an "intelligence community assessment" entitled "Assessing Russian Activities and Intentions in Recent US Elections" was released. Much of the alleged activities involved the acquisition of private data in the interest of damaging the security of the United States by disrupting or influencing the 2016 presidential elections. The report concluded that Russian intelligence, under the direction of Russian president Vladimir Putin, aspired to help then-President-elect Trump's election chances when possible. All three major US intelligence agencies— the FBI, the CIA, and the NSA—concurred in the report's conclusion.

Domestic and International Security: Hacking and Counter-Hacking

It's hard to feel secure when private and government servers keep getting hacked. This has both domestic and international impacts, of course, and it seems to be getting worse instead of better. It seems that every week we read of huge data breaches, and we hear about companies leaving private data—sometimes PII—sitting unprotected on servers that are open, if not to the public, then certainly to any enterprising hacker.

NOTE: The largest hacks ever (at least, that we know about) may have been the 2013 hack of Yahoo, in which 3 billion records were compromised, and the 2014 Marriott hack, in which 500 million records were compromised. As some have said, "There are only two types of companies—those that know they've been compromised, and those that don't know." (Alternatively, "There are only two types of companies: those that have been hacked and those that will be.")

In 2013, for instance, giant retailer Target Corporation was the victim of a data breach that affected millions of its customers. The company, which was accused of disregarding the notification of its own contracted security service (thus failing to mitigate the breach early on), initially reported that 40 million customers had been affected, but then had to revise that figure upward to 110 million after realizing that the hackers had stolen information about 70 million additional people, including names, mailing addresses, phone numbers, and email addresses. Interestingly, the breach did not affect online customers; only in-store customers were victimized, because the company's point of sale (POS) software had been compromised by a malware program called **BlackPOS**. The hack was eventually found to have been perpetrated by criminals using credentials that had been stolen from the company's AC/HVAC vendor.

Not all hackers are after money or even "street cred"—some are trying to promote a social or political cause. These are **hacktivists**: hackers for a cause. Hacktivists aim to disrupt (but generally not destroy) the infrastructure of their perceived enemies. Perhaps the most famous (or infamous, depending on your perspective) hacktivist group is Anonymous, which first gained fame after attacking the Church of Scientology and then the Ku Klux Klan, threatening to release the names of up to 1,000 members of the Klan and affiliated groups. Anonymous also attacked government agencies of the United States and Israel, the Islamic State of Iraq and the Levant (ISIS), child pornography sites, and the Westboro Baptist Church. The group seems to have gone into decline since its early 2000s heyday, with some subgroups splintering off the main body of the collective and some individuals deciding to operate on their own.

One question always comes up when discussing hacking, counter-hacking, and hacktivism: at what point do such attacks cross the line into cyberterrorism? The answer to that may depend on your ideological perspective—and on how you feel about whoever's being hacked. In general, a hacktivist does not seek to destroy infrastructure (physical or otherwise); hacktivism is merely disruptive, while the aim of cyberterrorism is to cause great harm, or inflict severe economic damage or even death. (Both types of hacking, mind you, are illegal.) Hacktivists seek to effect social change, while cyberterrorists seek terrorize by destroying people, countries, and infrastructure.

A related issue is **counter-hacking**, or "hacking back." The urge to counter a hacking attack by hacking back at the perpetrator is understandable, but the act is illegal. The (1984) **Computer Fraud and Abuse Act** outlaws almost any form of unauthorized access or access with ill intent, including intrusions from local or foreign sources, government systems, departments, and financial institutions and organizations. Put simply, the act outlaws *all* forms of hacking, and that includes counter-hacking.

There are good reasons for making counter-hacking illegal. For one thing, you cannot be positive of the identity of the hacker. Even if you could, you need to consider that hackers often route their attacks through the machines of innocent third parties. Thus, you could be hacking—or even damaging a system belonging to—an innocent bystander. This also applies to state-sponsored hacking. For instance, North Korea could route an attack through a group of Pakistani computers. If we counter-hack the Pakistanis, we're not attacking the actual source of the original attack.

Interestingly, if you are hacked and you know the source, the US Dept. of Justice recommends that you contact the system administrator from the attacking computer to request assistance. Oddly, this often works, because chances are that the system administrator is unaware that his or her network is being used to mount an attack, and will take steps to shut the hacker down.

The creation of hacking exploits has, not surprisingly, led to a digital arms war in which hacking exploits are collected, weaponized, and sometimes sold to the highest bidder. This includes exploits created by intelligence agencies, which sometimes lose control of their code so that it ends up on the open market. The 2017 **Protecting Our Ability to Counter Hacking (PATCH) Act** would have attempted to mitigate this problem by forcing the government to turn over its stockpile of offensive exploits, such as the NSA tool that was stolen, leaked, and then used to attack thousands of computers around the world, including Russia and the UK. The act was tabled and died in 2018.

Information Warfare

Information warfare is the weaponized use of information (or misinformation) to create a strategic or tactical advantage. Generally, it is thought to include the assumption that the target is unaware that the information being received has been manipulated. Not surprisingly, with the development of technology-abetted communicative systems (email, social networking, blogs, websites, etc.), the incidence of information warfare has been augmented and amplified by those systems. We have democratized information, but we have also democratized *mis*information.

Some of that misinformation doesn't even come from humans. A **bot** (short for "web robot") is a fairly simple piece of software that runs on a network or social network. It can be used to automatically tweet or retweet or like or unlike a post, or follow or unfollow a person. It can also be used to share posts—including its own posts.

There's nothing inherently wrong with, say, a Twitter-bot, and they are allowed on social networks as long as they follow certain rules. Over 25% of the tweets on Twitter are said to have been bot-created. Bots are well-suited to performing simple, repeatable tasks, and they're often used on social media networks, often by the network itself. They're also used to spread positive information about celebrities, businesspeople, product brands, and politicians.

NOTE: Republican and Democratic candidates both used bots in the 2016 election, with President Trump's campaign organization sending out about four times as many bot-created tweets as Hillary Clinton's team.

Unfortunately, bots can also be used to inflate the supposed appeal of a candidate (or product), and they can spread misinformation, which then gets retweeted (or shared or liked) by recipients of the tweet who do not realize that the information in the tweet is untrue, misleading, or out of date. Once those malign posts or tweets get started, it's difficult to stop them or to convince others that their veracity is doubtful. (As someone who was probably *not* Mark Twain has said, "A lie can travel halfway around the world before the truth can get its boots on.")

Bots can work in conjunction with fake accounts, at least until the social network realizes that the accounts are fake and removes them. This can take some time, though: Facebook took down over two billion fake accounts between January and March 2019, but many of them had been operating for years. And there are currently *more* active fake accounts, accounting for about 5% of the total accounts on the platform. Twitter has the same problem, with millions of fake accounts spreading information (and misinformation). Like Facebook, Twitter has removed millions of fake accounts, including fake bot-driven accounts, some of which attacked President Trump, and some that defended him. The company said in 2018 that it had removed more than 50,000 Russian-linked accounts from the social network.

As noted earlier, some ethicists feel that there are no new ethical issues, merely existing ones that have been updated—and often exacerbated—by technology. Misinformation has always been around and has always been spread, but technology enables information (and misinformation) to spread very rapidly, and the technology does little to authenticate that information. When a social network has over two billion active members (as does Facebook), information can be spread very quickly to a huge number of people. Twitter has said that information posted by Russian bots during the run-up to the 2016 election reached at least 677,000 Americans; social networks are *very* effective communication tools.

> **NOTE:** Hoaxes and misinformation are nothing new. In 1957, the BBC reported on a "spaghetti harvest" in Switzerland and was soon inundated with calls from people wanting to know how to grow spaghetti. But it goes back much further than that, and the hoaxes have often been political in nature, even centuries ago: In a 1782 effort to drum up support for the Revolution, Benjamin Franklin created a fake issue of a newspaper that reported that the British had hired Native Americans to scalp colonists. The "fake news" was reprinted in papers throughout New England.

It's also possible that some of the fake accounts are "fake fakes." In other words, they were false flag operations tied to opponents and meant to discredit them. A **false flag** operation disguises the actual source of the misinformation, attributing it to someone else. For example, one candidate could create a false document and attribute it to another candidate in attempt to discredit him or her. This can be done in an attempt to discredit rival groups or create the appearance of enemies when none exist.

One good example of information warfare gone bad—if it can ever be said to have gone well—was the **Cambridge Analytica** scandal of 2016. The UK firm was accused of having worked on Donald Trump's presidential campaign. That would be bad enough, given that foreign entities are forbidden from working on or for US candidates, but in addition, the company was accused of utilizing "dirty tricks" in the process, as well as supposedly collaborating with Russian agents during the incident. (Interestingly—and germane to our discussion—it turned out that Cambridge Analytica had been compiling profiles on millions of American voters; those profiles were based largely upon data harvested from Facebook profiles.)

Information warfare is just that: a war with weaponized information being brought to bear on targets. While many philosophers and ethicists feel that there are times when a traditional war can be justified—that there is such a thing as a **just war**—can an *information* war also be just? This is a question with which a number of ethicists have struggled. Only a few people felt that WWII was an unjust war; given a Japanese attack during peacetime and Hitler's radically fascist nation-building, most felt that the United States had no honorable choice other than to declare war on the Axis powers.

If we presume the notion of an ethical "just war," then when we discuss ethics in technology, we have to address the question that naturally arises: Is there such a thing as a just war when it comes to *information* warfare or other cyberwar?

The answer to that, not surprisingly, depends on whom you ask. But many tech ethicists believe that the two things are different enough that the typical rationalizations for a "just" traditional war do not apply when it comes to information warfare.

In the first place, say critics of the "just cyberwar" theory, the risk for an attacker using information as a weapon is much less than for a traditional attacker; there is less at stake, and thus less to ensure that the attacker has thought long and hard before initiating this kind of conflict.

Secondly, there are a huge range of technologies at risk during an information-based cyberattack (or any cyberattack), including civilian technologies and infrastructures that, in a traditional war, might be considered off-limits to an attacker. Often, there is no way to differentiate between military and civilian targets in an information war—civilian technologies and infrastructures could easily be accidental victims of information warfare gone astray. (This also applies to other forms of cyberattack, of course.)

Finally, in any tech-based attack, it's difficult to assign accountability or to know exactly who is responsible for the attack. In a traditional war, one generally knows by whom they're being attacked; in a cyberwar of any sort, you may not even know who's attacking you.

For all of these reasons, and some others we've not yet discussed, many tech ethicists reject the "just war" hypothesis when it comes to information warfare or other types of cyberattacks.

Military spokespersons have considered the issue, and they're well aware of the potential problems with a cyberattack of whatever sort. Questioned in 2010 about the dangers and limits of various forms of military cyberattack—including information warfare-based attacks—that might damage civilian infrastructure, Lt. General Keith Alexander promised to seek to limit the attacks' impact on civilians, noting that just as in a traditional war, US forces would seek to minimize civilian casualties.

NOTE: Lt. General Alexander, who commanded the United States Cyber Command from 2010 to 2014, retired in 2014 and established a private-sector security firm.

Cyberterrorism

Security researcher and US Naval Postgraduate School professor Dorothy Denning described cyberterrorism as "the convergence of terrorism and cyberspace." In simple terms, **cyberterrorism** is politically motivated hacking or misinformation intended to result in loss of life or severe economic loss, or both.

Given that definition, it's not always easy to draw a clear line between hacking, hacktivism, and cyberterrorism, especially since your definition may be subtly (or not so subtly) influenced by your political perspective.

We can generally define cyberterrorism by intent, as did Dr. Denning: using the internet to threaten physical harm for ideological purposes is cyberterrorism. Deliberate disruption of computer systems and networks for those same purposes may also be deemed cyberterrorism. However, hacking for money or to affect social change does not rise to the level of cyberterrorism, regardless of the identity and ideology of the attackers.

Some acts that may not cause *immediate* damage have also been deemed cyberterrorism, such as Al-Qaeda's utilization of the internet to communicate with and recruit new members. The ultimate goal of such recruitment is presumed ultimately to be physical harm and severe disruption of infrastructure.

If we use Denning's definition and take into consideration the cyberterrorism examples presented, then someone may have been guilty of cyberterrorism when Stuxnet was created. **Stuxnet** is a worm/virus that targets industrial systems; it was used to cause large-scale damage to Iran's nuclear program. The worm was believed to be jointly built by the US and Israel, though neither has admitted creating it. This is a good example of the part that political perspective plays in defining cyberterrorism: If "the other guy" does it, is it cyberterrorism? If *we* do it, is it cyberterrorism, or is it part of the "just war" we discussed earlier?

Extremist ideology of all sorts is getting a boost from social networking. As we've noted, social media is an amplifier—for good and bad. On the bad side, social media provides a convenient communication mechanism that seems to amplify anger and distortions of all types, even as it helps to spread misinformation. (Some of this may be due to the disinhibition effect we discussed earlier: it's simply easier to say hateful things when safely hidden behind a digital wall of anonymity.) This makes social media an all-too-frequent unwitting collaborator in various types of attacks. In 2019, for example, a 17-year-old high school dropout and two friends were arrested, accused of using social media to plan an attack on Islamberg, a Muslim settlement in upstate New York. That same year, right-wing extremist Brenton Tarrant not only planned and communicated about his attack on a mosque in Christchurch, NZ, he actually live-streamed part of the attack on Facebook. In 2017, a pro-Muslim extremist and former US Marine named Everitt Aaron Jameson was arrested after "liking" pro-Islamic State and pro-terrorism posts, and noting that he was planning a Christmas attack in San Francisco. In many cases, social media has unwittingly abetted the radicalization of disaffected young people on all ends of the political spectrum.

NOTE: Jameson eventually pleaded guilty to providing material support to the Islamic State of Iraq and was sentenced to 15 years in prison.

These days, Facebook and the other social networking sites are part of the everyday real world, and what happens there—including the amplification of hate speech and the radicalization of youth—cannot be separated from what happens "in real life." Many analysts feel that the ubiquity of the internet means that the chances of a cyberterrorist attack are greater than ever—and will continue to grow as the world becomes more connected. After all, a cyberattack is "cheap" in every sense: it's inexpensive to mount and there is no risk to a country's soldiers. Many times, as we've seen, it's not even possible to determine who mounted the attack, so the risk of counterattack is often minimal.

It's interesting to note that it wasn't until 2016 that the United States Department of Justice actually charged someone with cyberterrorism. Ardit Ferizi, a citizen of Kosovo, was charged with and convicted of hacking into a military website and passing a list of US military personnel to ISIL. (The White House may have had a hand in—and was certainly informed of—the arrest, but the post of White House Cybersecurity Coordinator has been eliminated in an attempt by National Security Advisor John R. Bolton to reduce layers of bureaucracy.)

Cyberterrorism sounds like science fiction—indeed, it has been a staple of science fiction for many years—but it's very real and its effects are very concrete. In 2007, someone (a state-sponsored entity believed but not proven to be in the employ of Russia) hit the Baltic state of Estonia with a massive denial of service attack. A **denial of service (DoS)** attack is among the simplest of cyberattacks: a computer simply sends, and keeps sending, requests to a server or group of servers until the servers are so overwhelmed that they cannot function and cannot respond to legitimate requests. The attack disrupted the entire country, including banking, cellular phone service, and access to healthcare information. Since much of the country's infrastructure is reliant on the internet, the entire country ground to a halt and the attack caused turmoil throughout the region.

NOTE: A *distributed* denial of service (DDoS) attack is one that enlists the help of many bot-controlled devices or computers to launch the attack.

The United States has not yet been seriously damaged by a true cyberattack, but some worry that it could happen, citing fears that many government networks and the private networks controlling the infrastructure (power, banking, utilities) are old and outdated. If so, it may be that the country's computer-controlled infrastructure is in no condition to stand up to such an attack.

Other countries *have* been victims of cyberattack. As noted earlier, much of Estonia was disrupted after a 2007 attack by state actors believed to be in the employ of Russia. In 2013, South Korea suffered a cyberattack that shut down three of its TV stations and impacted a bank. Though it's never been proven, it is assumed that the attack was perpetrated by North Korea. In March 2019, Indonesia's National Election Commission reported that Chinese and Russian hackers had probed Indonesia's voter database ahead of elections in that country; that same month, Iranian hackers targeted thousands of people at more than 200 oil-and-gas and heavy machinery companies across the world, stealing corporate secrets and wiping data from computers. In

February 2018, a cyberattack on the Pyeongchang Olympic Games took the official Olympic website offline for several hours and disrupted Wi-Fi and televisions at the Olympic stadium. (The attack was attributed to Russia.)

There's no shortage of examples of cyberattacks and preliminary probes that may presage cyberattacks. It may only be a matter of time before a crippling attack—or an attack intended to cripple—occurs.

LEGAL ISSUES IN CYBERSPACE

Free Speech

Democratic nations have always championed the idea of free speech, which the First Amendment guarantees to US citizens, while noting that there are certain limitations to that right. One cannot, as has often been said (by, among others, the United States Supreme Court in 1919) yell "fire" in a crowded theater. The right to free speech, the courts have said, does not extend to dangerous speech. However, what some have called "hate speech" *is* protected—at least up until the point at which it becomes dangerous.

Social networks have, at times, censored their subscribers' speech, deleting accounts or blocking posts that the network platform has deemed to have crossed an arbitrary line. In spite of the guarantee of free speech in the United States, this sort of censorship is perfectly legal, because social media platforms are private companies and are therefore free to censor if they choose to do so. Some have, in fact, objected that the social networks have not been quick enough to ban posts that contain harmful, dangerous content or have been characterized as hate speech containing incendiary content. In 2008, Democratic Senator—now former senator—Joseph Lieberman castigated YouTube for refusing to remove terrorist training videos. Shortly afterward, YouTube updated its community guidelines, warning that if such videos are uploaded to the service, individuals or accounts are at risk of violating the company's Terms of Service and could face permanent expulsion from the site.

Constitutional protections aside, when you post on social media, you are utilizing a free service provided by a company. With certain limitations, that company has the right to control what is communicated via its platform. When you signed up for the service, you agreed to the company's "Rules and Terms of Service." Those terms may preclude "targeted abuse," "harassment," or other types of posts.

Facebook's policy is to ban "individuals or organizations that promote or engage in violence and hate, regardless of ideology." In the spring of 2019, the company removed several people from its platform, portraying them (and their content) as dangerous. All content posted by Nation of Islam leader Louis Farrakhan, *Infowars* host Alex Jones, and conservative blogger/author Milo Yiannopoulos was removed.

Extremist groups of all stripes have faced not only social network bans, but also shutdowns by internet service providers (ISPs). For example, in spite of First Amendment guarantees of free speech, the neo-Nazi blog the *Daily Stormer* was barred by GoDaddy in 2017, its original service provider. The blog switched to the Google platform, but it wasn't long before it was banned by Google too. As we've noted, shutting down the blog was legal because both GoDaddy and Google are private companies, and are therefore free to censor the content on their platforms.

It's important to keep in mind that not all countries allow free speech. For example, a new law in Vietnam criminalizes criticism of the government. As a direct offshoot of that law, the Vietnamese government has required several things of social media companies operating in that country, including that the company must remove any content that the government deems offensive. Interestingly, the Vietnamese media hailed the government's actions, noting that those actions served to ensure "social order and safety." Then again, the media in Vietnam is run by the government and is unlikely to criticize the actions of that government.

Again, free speech does have its limitations. You're free to say what you want—on any platform you wish—but you're not immune to the consequences of your actions.

Some technology-abetted "free speech" crosses the line when it's used to attack people. **Doxing**, for instance, is a common method of attacking a person online. "Doxing someone" is the act of finding someone's publicly available information and posting it online; it is generally considered to be legal, so long as the information is publicly available. However, it's possible to uncover and publish private information, such as a social security number; that sort of doxing may be illegal. And even when the act itself is legal, the *precursors* to the act (e.g., how the data was obtained) and the *consequences* of the act (e.g., potential harassment, invasion of privacy, intimidation) may not be.

> **NOTE:** Like swatting, doxing can go terribly wrong. Following the 2013 Boston Marathon bombing, vigilantes on the Reddit social news/opinion forum wrongly identified a number of people as suspects. Then-general manager Erik Martin issued an apology for the "online witch hunts and dangerous speculation" that took place on the website.

We've already discussed swatting, which is when an attacker using the address of a target phones in a fake bomb report or other serious issue requiring a police presence in an effort to get the police to show up, ready to force entry to the target's home or office. Some might argue this is an example of free speech, but most would agree that it's dangerous speech, almost exactly akin to yelling "fire" in a crowded theater; death or injury are likely outcomes in both cases.

Hate speech is on the rise. According to the Southern Poverty Law Center, the number of websites featuring hate speech increased about 250% between 1995 and 2000. How much of this increase is attributable to social media and the internet is anyone's guess, but there's no denying that technology acts as both incubator and amplifier for *all* ideas, good and bad.

Online hate speech and intimidation are not new. In February 1999, a US District Court jury in Oregon awarded a group of doctors and clinics about $118 million (eventually reduced to $4.7 million) in a case that pitted abortion foes against doctors who performed abortions. The case mainly hinged on a website called *Nuremberg Files*, which published what the jury said amounted to a "hit list." The site published doctors' names and addresses on "wanted posters" decorated with dripping blood and pictures of dead fetuses, and it also published the names and ages of the doctors' spouses and children. People on both sides of the debate (which still rages on) agreed that calling for the murder of doctors and their families, which is what the site was accused of doing, was a step too far. The group's ISP shut down the site a few days after the site's founders lost a lawsuit filed by the ACLU and others.

Even when most agree that a particular example is hateful, removing that speech can still stir up argument. In response to social media companies' removal of what was called "terrorist propaganda," the *Washington Post* noted that citizens ". . . deserve to know what is going on in the world . . . however hard that is to stomach." The *Post's* argument echoes that of some human rights activists, maintaining that even if you consider something hateful and extremist, its very existence "adds valuable information to public discourse: the fact that such views exist can highlight the need to counter them."

Free speech issues can get mired in politics, of course, and one person's hate speech is another person's truth. So-called fake news is a good example. Is it satire? It is truth? Is it a lie passing itself off as truth? And if the latter, does that mean it's not protected by free speech guarantees?

Some countries are clamping down on fake news. In November 2018, the government of France passed an "anti-fake news" law that authorizes the immediate removal of "fake news" during election campaigns. In spite of arguments that such a law could jeopardize democracy and censor the press, the government's new law essentially regulates the internet.

> **NOTE:** The French law also allows the French national broadcasting agency to suspend television channels "controlled by a foreign state or under the influence" of that state if they disseminate false information that might affect the election results.

The risk here is that governments could tighten controls over citizens' data and use claims of "fake news" to justify suppressing dissent. Again, it depends on how we define "fake news" and on how that news is perceived; if it comes from a source you trust, you're likely to believe it and decry opponents' attempts to ban it. (See the discussion of the "liar's dividend" below.)

Other countries have also passed strict hate speech laws, and as a way of ensuring that American tech companies heed European laws relating to the removal of proscribed speech, some European countries have passed or threatened to pass laws making the companies liable for extremist speech. Up to this point, tech companies have not been held liable for what their users have said or posted on the internet.

Worldwide, free speech issues have been of concern to international groups. Article 19 of the International Covenant on Civil and Political Rights allows wide-ranging freedom of speech, irrespective of the media used. The United States, Switzerland, and Russia, among others, are all signatories.

Still, freedom of speech—on the internet, at least—varies widely. According to Freedom House, the five countries with the most internet freedom— measured to a great extent by their willingness to allow free, uncensored speech—were Iceland, Estonia, Canada, Germany, and Australia. The

United States was ranked 6th, which actually represented a slight decline that was partly attributed to the repeal of net neutrality laws. The biggest offenders, according to the report, were China, Iran, and Syria.

Just as the debate about privacy versus security can be summed up as a tension between citizens' rights to data and national security, the ethical dilemma over free speech on the internet can be summed up as the tension between citizens' rights to champion their viewpoints and society's right to be protected from what they find abhorrent views—especially views that might become dangerous rhetoric that could incite violence. We'll find many examples of such tensions as we examine the topic of ethics in technology, and ethicists say that this is why there are ethical dilemmas: most boil down to a tension between two opposing forces, each of which is valid in a certain context and to a certain degree.

Privacy Legislation and Industry Self-Regulation

People in the US (and elsewhere) demand a certain amount of privacy, and the Constitution seems to imply that they deserve privacy—though nowhere does the Constitution explicitly *guarantee* that privacy. The right to privacy, say many, is implied in the Fourth Amendment: "The right of the people to be secure in their persons, houses, papers, and effects, against unreasonable searches and seizures, shall not be violated, and no Warrants shall issue, but upon probable cause, supported by Oath . . . ." The Ninth Amendment, meanwhile, states that the "enumeration of certain rights" in the Bill of Rights "shall not be construed to deny or disparage other rights retained by the people." Some have interpreted that as a justification for presuming that the Bill of Rights protects privacy in ways not specifically provided in the first eight amendments. The Fourteenth Amendment's language ("No State shall make or enforce any law which shall abridge the privileges or immunities of citizens of the United States; nor shall any State deprive any person of life, liberty, or property . . .") has also been interpreted as alluding to an implicit guarantee of privacy.

> **NOTE:** Keep in mind that nowhere does the US Constitution guarantee a right to privacy. It's customarily assumed—and perhaps implied by certain amendments—but not explicitly guaranteed.

Explicit or implicit, the notion that people are deserving of a certain measure of privacy has become a common one, and US citizens have come to expect that their privacy will be respected and protected.

Online, though, our supposed guarantee of privacy seems flimsy. The technology is such that it's difficult to protect privacy online; there are too many data breaches, website scrapers, and scammers for us to feel that the guarantee is worth much. It also doesn't help that we willingly post private data—or information that could help others uncover private data—on websites, blogs, social networks, and in emails that are often read by providers and third-party developers working with those providers.

So, in order to protect some measure of our online privacy, two forces have stepped up to ensure that our data is not overshared or shared inappropriately: governments and the tech industry itself.

The industry, of course, would like to ensure that its customers' data remains safe, but the first duty of these companies, after all, is a fiduciary one. Above all else, they owe their shareholders whatever it takes to generate a profit. If profit and privacy come into conflict, we can assume that profit will almost always come first. The companies' devotion to privacy may be, as Hamlet said, "more honored in the breech than the observance."

Facebook, for example, has recently pledged an "about face" in its seeming disregard for subscribers' privacy, but the effectiveness of that pledge remains to be seen. In the meantime, the company has done a poor job of protecting users' privacy. (Then again, the whole point of Facebook is to share information about people, and most of that information is placed online by people using the service.)

At one point, the industry came up with **TrustArc** (originally TRUSTe), a for-profit privacy-enhancing body. TRUSTe was founded as a nonprofit industry association in 1997. One of its goals is to ensure that commercial websites adhere to their advertised privacy policies. The company provides "trustmarks" that serve as a visual guarantee to users that their privacy will be protected. The company also provides services to help corporations update their privacy management processes so they comply with government laws and best practices. Critics of the approach argue that voluntary schemes like this do not go far enough in protecting users' data.

As far as government efforts to safeguard privacy, there are state laws that address the issue, but there is no single overarching federal statute that covers all aspects of privacy or applies in all states. While the FTC regulates unfair commercial practices, including any misuse of private data, it's still mostly up to the states to provide privacy safeguards for their citizens.

Some countries have enacted laws that aim to protect people by allowing individuals to have personal information about themselves removed from the internet. The version of the **General Data Protection Regulation (GDPR)** adopted by the EU's member-states in 2016 guarantees the "right to erasure," though it specifies limits to that right. "Right to erasure" laws aim to protect people by allowing them to have information about themselves removed from the internet.

While there is no comprehensive federal privacy statute, several federal laws have been passed that do impact one or more aspects of privacy. Notable laws are listed in the following table.

Federal Laws Impacting Privacy

Legislation	Date	Privacy Protection
Family Educational Rights and Privacy Act (FERPA)	1974	Protects the privacy of student records.
Computer Fraud and Abuse Act (CFAA)	1984	Outlaws various types of online fraud, including trafficking in passwords, and prohibits even unintentional damage if "reckless disregard" is shown. The act has been amended several times since 1984.
Children's Online Privacy Protection Act (COPPA)	1998	Attempts to protect children from predatory or intrusive acts by websites collecting information about young users.
Controlling the Assault of Non-Solicited Pornography and Marketing (CAN-SPAM) Act	2003	Governs the sending of unsolicited commercial emails and prohibits deceptive subject lines in emails.
Fair and Accurate Credit Transactions Act (FACTA)	2003	An amendment to the Fair Credit Reporting Act that requires financial institutions and creditors to maintain written identity theft prevention programs in an effort to guard against identity theft.

There was a time when official DMV records were fairly easy to access, but that changed after a young actress named Rebecca Schaeffer was murdered in 1989 by a fan who located her through DMV records. As a result of that murder, the **Driver's Privacy Protection Act** was passed in 1994; it governs the privacy and disclosure of personal information gathered by state Departments of Motor Vehicles.

All 50 states (plus Puerto Rico, the District of Columbia, and the US Virgin Islands) have passed laws intended to protect citizens' privacy. One of the most stringent is the 2018 **California Consumer Privacy Act (CCPA)**, intended to align the state's privacy laws with Europe's GDPR privacy requirements. However, the law applies only to companies with revenues in excess of $25 million, or to companies that earn revenue via the sale of personal information—but only if the companies earn more than half of their revenues by selling such data. The law applies to companies that possess the personal information of 50,000 or more consumers, regardless of whether they sell that information.

NOTE: You might think that your business will not be affected by CCPA if you're not located in the state of California, but you may be wrong. Regardless of where you're located, if you do business in the state of California, you may be subject to its provisions. Be sure to check whether your business falls under CCPA.

There could have been—and may still be—more state privacy laws enacted, but so far, more than 50 of the 70 ISP-related privacy/neutrality bills sent to the various state legislatures have failed. Several more are listed as pending.

Some cities are finding that more and more technologies are being viewed as potential privacy violations. One of these is facial recognition, a technology that police officers in San Francisco, CA are no longer allowed to use. A city ordinance notes that facial recognition technology could endanger civil rights and civil liberties, which would outweigh any benefits.

Nationwide, facial recognition has become a hot topic of late, both because of the technology itself and because of concerns over the ethical use of that technology. The **Commercial Facial Recognition Privacy Act**, introduced in March 2019, would prohibit commercial users of facial recognition technology from collecting and sharing data from consumers without their consent. However, analysts predict that the bill will fail due to lack of Congressional support.

In 2008, the state of Illinois, while not specifically targeting facial recognition, passed the state's **Biometric Information Privacy Act (BIPA)**. The act guards against the unlawful collection and storage of biometric information, which would include facial recognition data. (There are bills pending to exempt private entities from BIPA, so long as the company does not profit from the information.)

Facial recognition, valuable though it might be to law enforcement efforts, raises some significant ethical questions. In the first place, it's not entirely accurate—and it's *least* accurate on persons of color, women, or the young. If nothing else, this means that the technology—as it currently exists—would tend to discriminate against those groups. That could be problematic when the technology is used as part of law enforcement efforts to recognize and detain suspects.

Of course, if you're in a public space, you're fair game for any facial recognition that takes place in that public space. The United States Supreme Court has ruled many times that citizens in public places have no right to an expectation of privacy. But other questions arise, including worries about how—and with whom—that data might be shared.

Another concern for ethicists involves participants' "informed consent." After all, you cannot consent to your image being captured and manipulated if you're not aware that the technology is in use.

It's not just law enforcement that uses facial recognition or other potentially intrusive technologies; they're also being used by businesses. Giant British supermarket chain Tesco's has for years used a form of facial recognition at their gas stations to target ads at customers based on their estimated ages. More recently, the chain has plans to place facial recognition technology at their self-checkout kiosks; the company is seeking ways to estimate the age of customers purchasing cigarettes, liquor, and other items that formerly might have required an employee to step in and approve the purchase. Facebook uses facial recognition to link users to their photos, Apple uses the technology in its "Memories" app, and Saks Fifth Avenue is using the technology in its Canadian stores.

Facial recognition has also invaded sports—or at least, sports stadia. In 2001, Super Bowl XXXV became known as the "Snooper Bowl," after local police deployed facial recognition technology and scanned the faces of stadium visitors, checking each face against a database of "troublemakers," including pickpockets, scam artists, and terrorists.

Not surprisingly, the federal government has an interest in the development of new and better facial recognition technologies. The **IARPA–Janus initiative** is an advanced research program sponsored by the United States Director of National Intelligence, aimed at developing such systems. The program is aimed at improving the current performance of face recognition tools by combining information captured by "media in the wild."

In the end, it's no surprise that securing our privacy is problematic, given that we're making such widespread use of so many technologies whose purpose is not to secure information, but to share it.

Intellectual Property

The idea of intellectual property (or IP) has been around for centuries, but the term itself became common only during the 20th century. It's a category of property that includes intangible creations: trademarks, patents, designs, and more. It refers, naturally, to creations of the intellect such as books, plays, artwork, and software, among others. IP laws exist to protect the creators of such properties so that they can realize an economic benefit—at least for some limited period of years—for their efforts.

> **NOTE:** In addition to IP rights, you may also have rights in tangible properties. If you buy a house or a car or a bag of groceries, those belong to you; no one is allowed to take them from you, and if they do, you have legal recourse.

Even before computers and the internet, intellectual property rights were at risk: it's not all that difficult to copy a printed book, write a "new" song based on an existing melody, or make a movie of a movie, for example. But with the advent of digital technologies, intellectual property issues have taken on a whole new dimension: It's now possible to copy nearly any intellectual property almost instantly, and making copies of those copies degrades neither the original nor subsequent copies—unlike photocopying a play, poem, or book, or making an analog tape duplicate of a song or album. This is great news for consumers of content, but not such good news for creators of that content; the ability to duplicate (and reduplicate) digital content makes it difficult for holders of IP rights to guarantee that they will receive their due based on their creative effort.

Not surprisingly, this brings up a host of ethical and legal considerations: Is it legal to make copies of someone's work? Is it *right* to do so? What are the limits of the protections offered by IP laws? Am I allowed to make copies of something (a book, a song, a piece of software) if I do it for my own use only? Can I legally give those copies away?

Usually, the law is fairly straightforward. If someone copies and distributes software, for example, he or she is almost always in violation of copyright. Similarly, if you copy a photo from the internet and paste it into your own work (a book, a blog, a website, etc.), that would almost always be a violation of copyright laws. Adding a photo credit does not excuse your use of someone else's intellectual property. If you copy a photo or a video clip and add a credit line that says something like, "All rights belong to the photographer" or "I do not own the rights to this music. Copyright by [name of copyright holder]," you have done absolutely nothing except show to the world (and the courts) that you knew you were committing a crime when you copied and pasted someone else's work.

There are occasions, though, when it is permissible to use someone else's work. One of those occasions is if the work is in the public domain. Works created prior to the existence of copyright law are in the public domain. So are works whose copyright has expired (works created after January 1, 1978, are copyrighted for the life of the author plus 70 years) or whose creator has purposely placed them in the public domain. (Note that the term of copyright for works created prior to 1978 varies, but a 27-year renewable term was typical.) Most government-sponsored works (photos, drawings, tables, etc.) are in the public domain, but that can vary, since the authors or photographers may also have rights in such properties, depending on the terms of the contracts under which they worked.

Another way to use someone's IP legally is to get permission, but be sure that you're getting permission from the correct person. A publisher, for example, may not hold the copyright to a book; it may be held by the author (or vice versa). Rights to a modern work of art obviously belong to the artist (or his or her estate) unless the art is in the public domain, but rights to a *photo* of a work of art almost always belong to the photographer; you don't have permission to duplicate the photo simply because it's a photo of something that may be in the public domain. The same goes for a recording of a Beethoven sonata; Beethoven no longer has any rights in the work, but the orchestra that recorded the sonata may.

One final way to use someone else's IP legally is to take advantage of the "fair use" clause of the **Copyright Act of 1976**. That clause notes that teachers, writers, critics, and others can use portions of copyrighted works in certain circumstances. One of those circumstances is in education, another is in critical or analytic works that, by definition, must duplicate some portion of the original work.

The "fair use" clause has limits, though. The courts generally apply a four-factor test to determine whether the use is justified. The court will consider: (1) the purpose and character of the use, including whether the use is commercial or nonprofit; (2) the nature of the copyrighted work; (3) the potential effect of the use on the IP rights holder's market; and (4) the "amount and substantiality" of the portion used in relation to the copyrighted work (e.g., if you use 90% of someone else's novel in your novel, you're probably not going to satisfy the fair use requirements).

Fair use (and copyright law in general) are far beyond the scope of our discussion, so be sure to get qualified advice if you intend to use someone else's work in any form.

One final way to use another's intellectual property is to license it. You can pay for a license, of course, depending on whether the copyright holder wishes to license the work. You can also use works licensed under such things as the Creative Commons Attribution-Share Alike 2.0 Generic license, often attached to media found on such sites as Wikipedia. You'll need to be sure that you're abiding by the terms of the license; many require that a credit line and/or the name of the license be included, and some require that the user include a link to that license or to the work or both.

There are those who have argued that software, at any rate, should be free—not necessarily free of charge, but free in the sense that that users should have the freedom to run the software, to study and change the software, and to redistribute copies at will, with or without changes. Richard Stallman's **Free Software Movement (FSM)** has championed this idea.

The idea of "freeware," though it sounds similar to Stallman's FSM, is somewhat different. With **freeware**, you are generally free to use and to share the software, but you cannot change it, nor can you charge for it.

Open-source software, meanwhile, can be free or fee-based, and it includes the source code, so that users are able to modify the software and distribute the modified versions of that software. The features added via modification are, in fact, sometimes used to justify charging for the software, as is expanded technical support for users.

In addition to the aforementioned Copyright Act, there are other laws that govern intellectual property issues, and some that attempt to address the changes that technology has wrought in this area. One of those is the 1998 **Digital Millennium Copyright Act (DMCA)**, which criminalized technologies that attempt to circumvent various forms of **digital rights management (DRM)**—i.e., copy protection. Since courts had previously said that it was perfectly legal to create archival or backup copies of software, movies, or other digital materials, the law created an ironic situation: according to the DMCA, it was illegal to circumvent the copy protection that was keeping users from copying materials that the courts had said they had a right to copy. The Librarian of Congress can issue exemptions to the law but, as you can guess, those are few and far between. One other important impact of the DMCA was that it shielded ISPs and other intermediaries from both direct and indirect liabilities, meaning that they could not be held responsible for what was published by those using their services.

There have been sporadic attempts to find ways around some of these laws. Perhaps the most notable—or at least, the one that brought the issue to the public's attention—was Napster, a peer-to-peer music service that briefly flourished in the late 1990s and very early 2000s. The idea behind Napster was a clever one: each subscriber accessed MP3 files stored on other subscribers' computers. Napster argued that this was perfectly legal because no one actually *copied* anything, and no one actually *distributed* illegal copies of songs. Several musicians and record companies disagreed and filed suit. Ultimately, Napster lost the suits, and in 2001 agreed to pay a $26 million settlement for unauthorized uses of music. The settlement included a $10 million advance against future licensing royalties.

It's even possible to inadvertently violate copyright, and one group came close. In the 1980s, a group called High Frontier made fun of President Ronald Reagan's Strategic Defense Initiative (SDI) by calling it "Star Wars." Lucasfilm (the creators of the *Star Wars* movies) filed suit, but lost when the court determined that use of the phrase was permitted so long as the group was not offering products or services using the name.

NOTE: Be very careful about loading illegal copies of software on your work computer(s). IT staff often keep automated running inventories that track what is (legally) installed on each workstation in the office; they have to do this because the company does not want to be held liable for copyright infringement just because you installed a "borrowed" copy of Microsoft Office on your work machine. You will be told to remove the software (or it may be removed for you) and you may suffer legal and other consequences.

The ethical issue here centers on the fact that, although it is illegal (and ethically suspect) to make use of someone else's intellectual property, modern technology makes it so simple to do that it's easy for us to convince ourselves that it must be permitted. It's not. This is another one of those "tensions" we've discussed, but in the end, it's simply wrong to steal, and that's what this is. If you use someone else's photograph, words, drawing, or whatever, you're stealing. Most ethicists (and courts) would agree that, understandable temptation aside, it's wrong.

Lawful Access and Encryption

Naturally enough, you have access to your data. If it's on your phone or on your computer, you can get at it. That data may be encrypted—or your device password-protected—so that no one else can get at the data (in theory, at least), but the information is always accessible to you; even if the data is encrypted **at rest** (a technical term that describes data that's protected as it sits on a device, as opposed to during transmission), you can view it because the applications you use to view the data know how to decrypt it on-the-fly so that you can read the information. Another term, **end-to-end encryption**, describes data that is encrypted both at rest and "in motion."

Properly configured modern devices, in fact, are quite good at protecting data. You can set your phone to lock automatically, and to unlock only if the correct PIN or password is entered. You can do the same with your computer. Depending on the application, the data may actually be encrypted such that, even if someone did gain access to it, he or she could not actually view, read, or understand it.

And this is where the problem lies. Sometimes, intelligence or law enforcement agencies wish to view that data. Whether they suspect you (or an associate) of a crime, or whether they're seeking confirmation of your location at a particular day or time, intelligence and law enforcement agencies often seek what is known as **lawful access**. They claim, often with good reason, to need access to that information in order to prevent or solve a crime or to prevent a terrorist attack. Often, they need access to the information quickly and without a warrant. It's important to note here that police and intelligence agencies often have different goals: law enforcement agencies might be focused on obtaining access to information to aid in prosecution; intelligence agencies often concentrate on preventing crime and terrorism. Either way, both are seeking lawful access.

As we've seen, there are good reasons for authorities to seek lawful access. Terrorists encrypt data too, as do hate groups and criminals of all sorts. The inability to lawfully access encrypted data, say supporters of lawful access, hinders law enforcement agencies' abilities to protect communities. What if a terrorist's captured smart phone contained information that might lead to his capture and avoid the deaths of hundreds of people? Would we not want law enforcement to be able to access that data? The agencies have characterized locked devices as having "gone dark." There is no way to access them, no way to view information that might save a life, solve a crime, or prevent an attack.

But not everyone agrees with the idea of lawful access. Some privacy activists believe that authorizing access (especially warrantless access) to encrypted data may increase the risk of *unauthorized* government access to that data. And aside from the possibility of government agencies overstepping their bounds, technologists worry that that once a "key" or "back door" is provided for law enforcement, it will inevitably find its way into the hands of others—information is porous; it is its nature to leak when shared.

Some argue that granting lawful access could actually harm the economy, because people may be reluctant to purchase products or services from countries in which government agencies could have access to their private information and communications. And companies themselves may fear lawful access because they could stand to lose business: if a company does business in China, goes the argument, it might be reluctant to continue doing business there, because the government (and possibly competing Chinese companies) might have access to its trade secrets.

One argument against lawful access is that even absent such access, agencies can still examine **metadata**, which is data *about* the communication in question, such as time stamps, locations, dates, and more. Since metadata is rarely encrypted, some argue that it's almost as useful as the actual communication: metadata can often be used to determine where people were, who they were talking to, for how long, and at what time.

These are not merely theoretical issues. In a 2015 case involving Apple, Inc., a Pakistani husband and wife shot up and attempted to bomb a San Bernardino County Department of Public Health training event and Christmas party. Fourteen people were killed. After the killing of the attackers, the FBI announced that it was unable to unlock one of the phones it had recovered, due to the phone's security features. A court order was issued in an attempt to force Apple to unlock the phone, but Apple refused. Eventually, the Department of Justice dropped its suit, noting that it had been able to unlock the phone.

> **NOTE:** In the 2015 Apple case, it later turned out that the DOJ had contracted the services of an Israeli security company to hack into the phone.

Interestingly, the law that the FBI cited in its attempt to force Apple to comply with a court order to unlock the terrorists' phone was a very old one. The **All Writs Act of 1789** authorizes courts to compel third parties (e.g., Apple) to assist in the execution of a court order, and the FBI argued that the law, old though it might be, applied here.

Once again, the argument here comes down to a tension between a need for security (as provided by law enforcement and intelligence agencies) and data privacy (as provided by tech companies' data and device encryption). The tradeoff between security and privacy is again at the core of our ethical concerns. Could authorities misuse lawful access? Could others take advantage of it? How much security are we trading for how much data access?

Cybercrimes

Crime has always existed. But the advent of new technologies has created different forms of crime, spawned new avenues for criminals, and brought to the forefront new dimensions of ethical and legal issues.

One legal problem we encounter with cybercrime is that jurisdictional issues often arise. If someone stops you on the street and takes your wallet and watch, there's no confusion about where that crime occurred. The local police will seek a local criminal who committed a crime in their jurisdiction.

Cybercrimes are different, though. There are no clear boundaries in cyberspace: The criminal may be in one jurisdiction, and his or her data may be stored and transferred through multiple other jurisdictions. Meanwhile, the victim may be in yet another city, state, or country. Which law enforcement agency is in charge? How is a faceless criminal to be pursued through a maze of servers and proxy servers, some of which are in foreign countries? On which device was the crime even committed?

One crime that technology has certainly abetted is stalking. It's always been possible to stalk someone, but computers and the internet have made stalking easier, giving would-be stalkers immense power. Stalkers can use technology to harass another individual from the "comfort" of their own living room, keep track of the other person's whereabouts, and even read private messages to friends. And it's not hard to look up another person's address online or use computer-derived location data to attempt to stalk someone in real life (IRL). While it's not illegal to look up someone's location or address, and it's not illegal to walk down the street across from someone's home, it *is* illegal if the behavior becomes threatening or intimidating.

Another type of crime given new life by technology is extortion of various types. For example, if someone initiates a DDoS attack and then demands money to call off the attack, that's extortion.

Ransomware is a special kind of extortion that involves encrypting a victim's files and demanding a ransom to decrypt the files. Law enforcement agencies recommend not paying, but many do pay: if your business—which could be a bank, a hospital, or an entire city—has ground to a halt, you may feel that you have no choice but to pay up. There have been several high-profile examples of ransomware in the news: Hospitals in Los Angeles, CA, and Greenfield, IN, paid ransoms of $17,500 and $55,000, respectively, to get their establishments back up and treating patients. The cities of Atlanta, GA, and Baltimore, MD, were both hit with ransomware attacks in 2019; neither paid the ransom, but both will have spent millions of dollars by the time everything is restored, and their systems are running once again.

Even the police have fallen victim to ransomware. In 2018, the Lauderdale County Sheriff's Department in Meridian, MS, was hit, and a bit earlier in the year, the Lamar County Sheriff's Department in Purvis, MS, was a victim of a ransomware attack. Police agencies in Arkansas, Maine, and Missouri have also been victims of ransomware attacks.

Bullying is another activity that has been abetted by technology, and to the extent that it becomes harassment or intimidation, it too is a crime. Bullying has always been a fact of life; in school or in the neighborhood, some people simply like to pick on others and always have. But the pervasive reach of the internet now means that people (often, but not always, young people) can be bullied around the clock via text, email, or social media; people today are always connected and so are their bullies.

Problems such as theft, bullying, and stalking have always existed, which takes us back to one of our earlier questions: Does technology create *new* ethical issues, or does it simply exacerbate or change older ones? Bullying, as we've said, has always existed, but technology has changed it; it seems pretty obvious that this is an exacerbation of an old issue.

Cornell's Helen Nissenbaum would agree. She notes that these issues have always existed, but because of the technology-abetted erosion of privacy, the problem has become worse. Most would agree with her, but not all.

Some ethicists say that technology has indeed created new problems—or that it has changed the situation so drastically that they might as well be new problems.

James Moor, for example, believes that cyberethics issues are unique because they've been created by unique technology. A computer, he says, is **logically malleable**. That is, rather than being created for a single purpose, a computer can be instructed to do many things; therefore, says Moor, it creates "new possibilities for human action." It also creates what Moor called "policy vacuums" and "conceptual muddles" because the technology can be used in unanticipated ways for unanticipated purposes.

NOTE: James Moor is a philosophy professor at Dartmouth College and is the former editor of the journal, *Minds and Machines*. He is the author of *The Turing Test: The Elusive Standard of Artificial Intelligence*, among other publications.

Ethicist Walter Maner, a former chair of the Department of Computer Science at Bowling Green State University, agrees with Moor, though his reasoning is somewhat different. Maner feels that, if nothing else, technology-related ethical issues must be viewed as unique simply because the technology is uniquely fast and uniquely complex.

TECHNOLOGICAL INNOVATION AND ETHICS

Biotechnologies

Developments in biotechnology create opportunities for increased lifespan, new treatments for diseases, and a better life for many, but they also present challenges by stretching ethical boundaries and forcing us to ask important questions: How much are we permitted to tinker with the body? With genes? With the essence of life itself? What constitutes responsible research? To what extent must researchers protect the privacy of subjects? Should stem cell research be allowed? What types of stem cell research?

What role does the potential for bioterrorism play in our research, our preparations, and our goals? Are things created in a lab (meat, grains, animals—even humans, someday) the same as the original things? Or are they different and thus subject to different ethical considerations?

NOTE: Questions about the ethics of biotechnology are not new. Many of them were examined in Mary Shelley's *Frankenstein*, a book from which much subsequent science fiction could be said to derive. The questions were old even in 1818, when Shelley wrote the book.

In July 1996, a lamb was born in Midlothian, Scotland. One would not think that the birth of a lamb would have much of an ethical impact, but the controversy that erupted around the world is still going strong. Dolly the sheep was the first mammal cloned from an adult cell. Is Dolly actually a "real" sheep? Can wool taken from Dolly be sold as wool, or must it be labeled differently? If Dolly were slaughtered for food (she wasn't), would the meat be sold the same as any other lamb or mutton? Or would it need different labeling?

NOTE: Dolly was euthanized in 2003, at the age of six, after tumors were discovered in her lungs.

Cloning humans would, of course, present its own set of ethical issues, one of which is dealing with the fact that there is a relatively high incidence of deaths and birth defects in cloned animals. Another is the fear that cloned children may be expected to live up to the achievements of their genetic predecessors. Perhaps the most alarming question is this: What if society (or some subgroup of society) decided to clone only the "desirable" people, for whatever purpose or reason? Who decides what constitutes "desirable"? And what does one do if he finds himself *not* among the desirables?

Of course, there are proponents of human cloning. They point out that, among other benefits, cloning could be a way to help prevent genetic disease or to provide offspring for infertile couples.

But this takes us back to one of our earlier questions: What do we *call* a cloned human? Is he or she human, or something else? Would the human equivalent of Dolly be allowed to vote? To own property? The question of what to call a cloned person is significant.

Let's take a look at some other cloning examples to help demonstrate the importance of labeling. We can now grow "meat" in a laboratory, which opens up a debate about labeling synthetic foods. The synthetic food labeling debate is not new, however. Dairy farmers in the 1870s railed against margarine and insisted that it be called and classified as something different—something nondairy. Since the lab-grown meat is actually slabs of protein cultured and grown from animal cells, the problem with not calling lab-grown meat "meat" is that—unlike the whole butter vs. margarine ruckus—cultured meat is actually biologically identical to the product we get from a cow, steer, or other animal. In this case, it *does* come from an animal—it's grown from cells taken from donor animals.

The argument over "fake meat" is more than merely a marketing issue—it goes to the heart of what we're able to call things. If lab-grown "meat" is determined not to be meat, then is a cloned person a person? Is a child who exists because of in vitro fertilization still a "real" baby? (By now, most agree that it is, in spite of the fact that it is a form of assisted pregnancy. But there were doubters early on, and many still view the practice with distaste.)

In the United States, both the FDA and the USDA are involved in the argument about meat, and they may not agree on whether lab-grown "meat" can in fact be called "meat." Both agencies have some responsibility related to the health of food and the accuracy of food labels, and this could cause jurisdictional issues. The FDA seems to be more lenient in terms of product names. The agency has allowed almond milk and soymilk products to use those names, despite pushback from the dairy industry. Recently it allowed an eggless mayo replacement to use the term "mayo" on its packaging, even though the agency's own standards define mayonnaise as something containing egg whites.

The labeling issue remains somewhat unsettled, which is not surprising, given that it involves politics, bureaucracy, marketing, and lobbying efforts on both sides.

Some of the same issues arise when we talk about **genetically modified organisms (GMO)**—seeds or plants that have been genetically modified to gain some advantageous trait: perhaps they're hardier, need less water, grow larger, or are more resistant to pesticides. Like Dolly or lab-grown "meat," GMO foods are different than the original strain. Does that mean they must be labeled differently? Are they as good as non-GMO foods? Are they food at all?

Like most arguments with an ethical component, the discussion about GMO foods is complex, nuanced, and contentious. Studies support both sides of the argument, so appealing to science for an answer is difficult. Proponents say that GMO foods are not only safe, but reduce hunger and poverty worldwide, while reducing the environmental impact of agriculture. Opponents say that genetic modifications are not in our best interests because they're associated with increased use of chemicals that contaminate soil and an increased use of pesticides.

Unsurprisingly, the arguments get even more strident when we stop talking about steak and plants and start talking about people. One issue that has arisen is the question of who has rights to blood and tissue samples taken from you during a medical procedure done in a US facility. You might think that those automatically belong to you, but you would be incorrect, as several court cases show.

One now-famous example is **Henrietta Lacks**, an African-American woman who died of cancer in 1951. Her name is attached to an ongoing ethical debate over bioethics, because doctors cultured her cells without her knowledge and used them for research. The cells were even commercialized—sold to cancer researchers. Lacks' family did not discover this until 1975. Today, researchers continue to culture (and sell) the HeLa line of cells in order to study them.

NOTE: In 2013, researchers actually published the DNA sequence of the genome of a strain of HeLa cells.

The Henrietta Lacks HeLa cell line question echoes previous topics in our ongoing discussion of ethics in technology. Ms. Lacks was not paid for the use of her cells. She wasn't even informed that they were being used, which brings up the issue of informed consent we've touched upon elsewhere. It's difficult to conceive of information that is more private than the cells of one's own body, but that privacy was seemingly violated. Lacks certainly lacked agency as far as the disposition of her cells was concerned.

The argument over who owns your cells continues. In 1990, a cancer patient named John Moore sued UCLA for using his cells and commercializing his cell line for research purposes. The California Supreme Court ruled that UCLA was free to use Moore's cells however it chose, including the creation of a commercialized cell line.

Cell cultures aside, no cell-related issue has raised hackles like the ongoing debate over the use of stem cells in research. This is especially true of the debate over the use of embryonic stem cells, the ethical issue being that such use can destroy the embryo. Since an embryo can develop into a human being—and since many consider that the embryo is already a human being—such research is highly controversial. Opponents of embryonic stem cell research argue that such research is tantamount to murder. The debate over the use of adult stem cells is much more muted, as is the use of one's own stem cells, since the destruction of an embryo is not involved.

One promising avenue of research that may somewhat mitigate—but will certainly not end—the fierce stem cell debate is the discovery of regular cells than can be induced to behave like embryonic stem cells. **Induced pluripotent stem (iPS) cells** are taken from adult donors and, like stem cells, can become any type of cell in the body. They are useful, though they cannot replace stem cells in every respect for all types of research.

Another medical procedure that has raised ethical questions is the harvesting of human eggs for research. Women take fertility drugs in order to produce enough eggs to be useful, and the drugs and the removal of the eggs can present risks. Should women undertake those risks? Should they be paid to produce eggs?

Biotechnological ethics concerns are not going away; in fact, as technology advances, we can be certain that more issues will arise. Researchers have **bioprinted** experimental skin replacements; one day, those might take the place of painful, expensive skin grafts needed for burn patients and others. Some bioprinting experimenters are using machines that look and act eerily like the inkjet or 3D printer you may have sitting on your desk at home. Printing a functioning transplant organ may not be many years down the road; already, doctors have printed a new bladder for a patient and transplanted it into the patient's body. As the science of bioprinting advances, would you have qualms about accepting a 3D-printed liver if you knew that it meant the difference between living and dying?

NOTE: At any given time, many thousands of people await organ transplants, but there is a shortage of such organs. Bioprinting 3D organs could help satisfy the demand, especially given that they can be printed using a patient's own cells, which would greatly reduce the possibility of organ rejection.

That last was not meant to be a flippant question. If we're to examine the ethics of various forms of technology, we must admit that it's possible to be against something on general ethical principles, and yet realize that we may feel quite differently when we are the ones benefitting from what we previously felt was an ethically questionable action. Being against a particular medical treatment or lab-gown food is easy, until it's you who is about to die or about to starve. That realization tends to call into question our entire ethical framework.

The Internet of Things

It's likely that the inventors of what would eventually become the internet didn't quite grasp the enormity of what they were unleashing upon the world. The forerunner of the internet, the **Advanced Research Projects Agency Network (ARPANET)**, was created under the auspices of the US Department of Defense. It was envisioned as a way to link universities and research teams together so that they could share information—and today, the internet is still about sharing information. (And not so much about protecting data, which is part of the reason that security is such a big issue.)

Not only did the scientists—people such as Leonard Kleinrock, Vinton Cerf, Bob Kahn, and J.C.R. Licklider (and Sir Tim Berners-Lee, who invented the web browser and HTML, giving rise to what we know as the World Wide Web)—not realize just how powerful and how ubiquitous the internet would become, they surely never envisioned all of the *things* we're connecting to the internet: thermostats, lighting systems, research equipment, watches, parking meters, locks, vehicles, street lamps, and more. We're even connecting animals to the internet, largely as a way to monitor their location and their health. Researchers estimate that by 2020 there are going to be 50 billion devices connected.

Thus, we have the **Internet of Things (IoT)**, which is commonly defined as the interconnected network of home and industrial devices that collect data from their environment, potentially react to that environment, and communicate that data over the internet, sometimes to other devices.

We wish, of course, to have personalized experiences with our interconnected devices, and that gives rise to both security and ethical problems: Digital assistants respond to our voices and keep our calendars for us. Our smart watches let us know if our hearts are behaving strangely. Our thermostats know what time we come home and when we awake. To get personalized experiences, we must give up personal information. What happens with that information is the crux of a number of ethical issues.

The IoT is based on real-time data collection and monitoring, and when data is collected and monitored, thorny questions emerge: Who owns that data? Who is being monitored? Do we know that an IoT device intended to monitor one thing is monitoring only that thing? What is being done with the collected data? Who has downstream access to it? What is the real value here, anyway? Is it the data to which our smart homes and utility meters and refrigerators respond? Or is the real value the aggregated data (the "big data") collected and mined by thermostat and appliance manufacturers, television manufacturers, utility companies, and others?

While many point to **radio-frequency identification (RFID)** chips (which were being demonstrated in the early 1970s) as the forerunner of the IoT, the IoT may be said to have truly begun in 1982, when a Coca Cola machine at Carnegie Mellon University was modified to report its own inventory and monitor the temperature of drinks. We've gone from one connected vending machine in 1982 to upwards of 50 billion such devices in 2020.

Keep in mind that 50 billion connected IoT devices means 50 billion devices' worth of data moving over the internet. That data has value; in fact, with that many devices and that much information, the data's aggregate value may be incalculable. Of course, whenever we connect something to the internet, we expose what cybersecurity researchers call an "attack vector," another potential security hole through which data can leak and hackers can enter. That means that by 2020, there will be another 50 billion security holes ready to be exploited by hackers and scammers. This is especially alarming given the fact that few IoT devices are well-secured; this is why we hear frequent reports of hacked baby monitors, routers, automated building systems, and (somewhat ironically) security cameras. Even more worrisome are reports of hacked medical devices—pacemakers and heart monitors—and vehicles.

We've noted that many IoT devices are easily hacked. One of the most infamous examples of this sort of hacking was the Mirai botnet attack in 2016. The attacks hit several different types of IoT devices, including webcams, DVRs, routers, and more. These devices are not very secure—and owners ensured that they were even less secure by not protecting them with strong passwords. The Mirai malware attacked via a **botnet** (a network of compromised computers and other devices), striking mainly through unsecured IoT devices such as those listed, and adding them to the number of devices under its control. The bot-controlled collection of devices then launched a DDoS attack in 2016 that brought down the entire internet on much of the East Coast and many regions of Brazil, Vietnam, and Columbia.

A less destructive example of potential problems with the IoT surfaced in 2016, when a "smart" sex toy was discovered to be collecting and communicating user data to the device's manufacturer. A woman sued the company, alleging that the manufacturer was "collecting information about her and other users' preferred vibration settings, the dates and times the device is used, [and] the email addresses of [device] owners who had registered their devices . . . [obtaining] all this data without the permission of its users." The class action suit was settled when the manufacturer agreed to pay $3.75 million to users.

The above example demonstrates a serious ethical issue to which we've already alluded to: What happens with data collected by IoT devices? Who owns it? For what purposes can it be used? In this case, the device wasn't hacked by some scammer; the data was collected and used by the manufacturer. Might other manufacturers collect—unbeknownst to device owners—data that might prove embarrassing or intrusive? Might they then (knowingly or unknowingly) share that data with others?

This takes us back to Nissenbaum's discussion of "contextual integrity." We might be agreeable to an IoT thermostat collecting temperature information and noting the times we awake so that the device can increase the heat a few minutes before we rise in the morning. But how would we feel if that data were stored on the manufacturer's server, where it might be vulnerable to a hacker who could view the data and know what time we rise for the day and what time we depart for work? Would we be comfortable if the manufacturer shared that data with, say, a marketing company seeking to sell products to people who rise late or are at home all day? As Nissenbaum notes, it's not so much the original data acquisition that's a potential problem, but who gets to see and use it after we've lost control of that data.

Government agencies have taken note of the possible benefits (and risks) of the IoT, and some have begun taking steps to ensure that the technology works as safely and effectively as possible. In 2017, the US Department of Commerce issued recommendations for IoT development. The agency recommended that IoT devices should be (1) stable, (2) secure, and (3) trustworthy. Note that these are merely *recommendations*; there are currently no federal laws addressing specific IoT issues, though California has passed SB-327, which attempts to address security issues in IoT devices.

No discussion of IoT, no matter how abbreviated, would be complete without mentioning devices like Amazon's Alexa digital assistant. Alexa may be the most ubiquitous example of IoT technology in the home. The device can answer questions, adjust your lights, open and close drapes, and much more. It can even purchase items on command—through Amazon, of course. The main worry about Alexa is that the device may be listening and collecting data without users' knowledge. Of course, Alexa *must* listen, but it's supposed to disregard everything it hears until it hears the wake word, "Alexa." But users worry that, since it's listening, it could be recording and sending to Amazon conversations not meant for Alexa. This has actually happened on rare occasions, but it's uncommon, and a huge array of variables have to be present in order to trigger this sort of thing—the most obvious being that a word that sounds like "Alexa" needs to have been uttered. Still, there have been anecdotal reports of Alexa users having mentioned products in their homes and then having those products turn up in various social network feeds or web ads.

Alexa *is* recording your requests; you can actually listen to—and delete—those recordings by going to Settings in the Alexa app. But there are fears, reasonable or not, that Amazon is using those audio recordings for more than merely training its systems to respond more quickly and accurately.

Of course, if you invite into your home an intelligent microphone connected to even more intelligent servers running sophisticated software, then you've invited into your home a series of potential security vulnerabilities. Can you trust Alexa? Probably. But more than 100 million Alexa devices have been sold, and those recordings are stored on Amazon's servers; they're no longer under your control, so you have no recourse if they were somehow to leak.

Alexa is a prominent example of a popular IoT device, but there are many, many others, and there are about to be millions more. The Internet of Things is a perfect example of technology that is meant to collect data; once it's collected, we may have little say in what happens to it next. Nissenbaum would say that the contextual integrity of that data has eroded; it is no longer under our control.

Robotics and Artificial Intelligence

Science fiction books and movies from *I, Robot* to *Bladerunner* to *Terminator* have introduced us to truly intelligent machines, and have posed a serious ethical quandary that we may someday have to consider: if a robot has a brain and thought processes equal to those of a human being, should it also have the legal rights—and the political rights—of a human being?

> **NOTE:** Many roboticists talk about the "uncanny valley," the relationship between how much a robot resembles a human being and our emotional response to that resemblance. Some researchers believe that we're quite comfortable with robots that do not look much like humans at all, and possibly also with robots that would look *exactly* like humans—should that ever become possible. But humans seem to have emotional problems with robots that look . . . not *quite* human; semi-human robots are apparently "off" just enough to make humans feel uncomfortable.

We're not there yet, but we're well on the way. Advances in robotics and artificial intelligence point to a burgeoning—and ever more sophisticated—robotics industry that, even now, is beginning to affect the way we live, work, and play.

One possible negative result of the robotics revolution is disruption to the workforce. Computers (and a robot is basically a mobile computer that interacts with its environment) are essentially "universal tools," as a result of what James Moor has called a computer's "logical malleability"; a computer can perform many tasks—perhaps almost any task. Computers don't get tired, they need no sleep, and they don't go home in the evening. As a result, computers have been seen as a threat to workers. Many fear they can be replaced by computers, and in countless cases this fear has been borne out.

The fear of new technology affecting jobs is nothing new. It goes back to the Luddites and before. In the 19th century, **Luddites**, English textile workers who had lost their jobs as new machinery took over the industry, protested the changes that technology was bringing to their industry. An entire protest movement—named after Ned Ludd, an 18th-century millworker—grew out of the workers' disillusionment over the changes technology were bringing to their industry. Today a Luddite is anyone who is opposed to new technologies, or to change in general.

Long before that, though, people were worried about being put out of work by machines. In the 16th century, Queen Elizabeth I refused to patent a knitting machine on the grounds that it would put many of her subjects out of work. (Some of Elizabeth I's concern might in fact have been politically motivated: she may have been responding to pressure from members of one or more of the artisan guilds that operated at that time.)

Even though the issue is not new, advancing technology—and its increasing sophistication—means that these kinds of disruptions in industries occur much more often than in previous times and impact more people more quickly than before. Partly this is due to **Moore's law**, named after former Intel CEO Gordon Moore, who noted that the number of transistors in an integrated circuit doubles every two years, even as the price gets lower and the circuits get smaller. The result has been an explosion in technology in general and in robotics and automation in particular.

Thus, technology has exacerbated an existing issue, and it's affecting all of us, one way or another. White collar workers, long thought to be immune to such changes, have in fact been one of the most affected groups. Mid-level white-collar workers with intermediate skills are finding that much of their work is now—or will soon be—performed by computer programs.

The effects of this sort of disruption are not all negative. While a large percentage of jobs (47%, say some researchers) will someday be automated, that very automation will free up workers for other types of work and will in fact create many jobs—possibly more jobs than it eliminates. It may even be that innovation is actually creating jobs more quickly than automation and technology are destroying them. These will be different jobs, though, in different industries than those in which many of us currently work. After all, someone has to build the machines, program them, maintain and repair them, design them, and erect the buildings in which all of this work will take place. Also, technology tends to create entirely new industries. Only a few years ago, there was no such thing as desktop publishing; only the very wealthy could start a magazine or a newspaper, but now just about anyone can become a "publisher." (This is not always for the better, of course.) Not long ago, there was no such thing as a vlogger, a roboticist, a YouTuber, a cybersecurity expert, an online fashion blogger, a data scientist, a podcaster, a home-based recording engineer, an online retailer, or an Uber driver.

So, while many workers have been replaced by computers and computerized devices, new jobs are being created. However, many workers fear that they may not have the opportunity to retrain for those jobs.

When a committee of the IEEE Robotics and Automation Society created a framework for addressing the ethical questions prompted by robotics research, the overall intent of the committee's recommendations was to ensure that robots and similar technologies are used responsibly. Given the 47% eventual automation figure noted above and PricewaterhouseCooper's estimate that some 30% of jobs will soon be automated, ethicists point out that part of a responsible approach to the new technologies should be to ensure that retraining and re-education will be readily available for those whose jobs have disappeared. These people may find themselves out of a job with little notice, and it's only fair that they're given retraining opportunities quickly. (And fairness is, after all, a cornerstone of ethics.)

One thing that researchers are not sure of is just how advanced AI (artificial intelligence) and robots could become. Some feel that AI and AI-equipped robots could approach—or even surpass—human intelligence in a relatively short period of time. If that's true, then the idea of truly intelligent machines poses the serious ethical quandary mentioned earlier: If a robot has a brain and thought processes equal to those of a human being, should it also have the legal rights—and the political rights—of a human being? And if the answer to that question is yes, that could mean that robots could have the right to vote and to own property, and could not be imprisoned or deprived of "life" without due process. (Interestingly, we must assume that if a robot has the same legal rights as a human, it cannot own another robot—since the second robot also has the same legal rights as a human. And even more interesting is the idea that it would also mean that a *human* could not own a robot.)

We're already beginning to see the results of some work in AI, and it's not always pretty. One of the most recent and perhaps most disturbing technological innovations has been the use of artificial intelligence to create "deepfakes." (The word comes from combining "fake" and "deep learning"—a form of artificial intelligence.) A **deepfake** is made by using AI to combine or superimpose images or videos to create fake videos of people doing or saying things they never actually did or said.

One needn't be an experienced programmer or AI researcher to create deepfakes. There are now software applications that allow nonprogrammers to create deepfakes. This development could portend an internet awash in fake videos of people doing and saying things they never really did or said. What are you supposed to do when you can no longer believe your eyes and ears? What happens to truth when you can no longer trust pictures, audio, or video of public persons, politicians, diplomats, or military officers?

But help in detecting AI-produced deepfakes is on the way, aided—somewhat ironically—by the same artificial intelligence used to create the fakes in the first place. In 2019, an organization known as ASVspoof.org sponsored an international challenge in which teams sought to develop software to detect audio fakes. Researchers are also working on AI-based software that can detect video deepfakes, and some hope to have the software available prior to the next presidential elections, when many fear that an avalanche of the fake videos will be released in an attempt to influence voters by showing political opponents doing or saying things that they never did or said.

AI-equipped weaponry is another concern, especially when it's designed to be autonomous. (And why else would such a weapon require an AI component, if not for autonomy?) A 2015 open letter signed by 25,000 artificial intelligence professionals requested that researchers and authorities ban autonomous weapons. The thought of a weapon that can decide on its own when (and what) to attack frightens many ethicists and more than a few scientists. The idea of **lethal autonomous weapons systems (LAWS)** that might someday work without human input seems, to many, like a dangerous line to cross.

But we've come quite close to crossing it already. LAWS have been invented and deployed—at least for testing—though they are currently under human supervision. In 2007, a semi-autonomous Oerlikon GDF-005 cannon being tested in South Africa malfunctioned; nine people died and 14 were injured. The exact cause of the accident was never determined, but it seemed to be due to either software or hardware problems. This is worrisome on several ethical fronts. First, we already know that hardware is imperfect, and that software is inherently buggy; the idea of entrusting a life-or-death decision to a possibly flawed machine frightens many. (Then again, people are currently in charge of advanced weaponry, and people are certainly flawed.) The other issue here has to do with accountability. With an autonomous or semi-autonomous weapon, we can't simply hold the machine responsible when something goes wrong, so who is accountable? The manufacturer? Hardware contractors? Software programmers? Whatever we decide, you can be sure that LAWS do (or will soon) exist; many nations are working on their development, and we could see an AI-based arms race in the near future.

Some researchers believe that we can make robots in our image. That is, we can make them *literally* in our image (they can be humanoid) and also *morally* in our image (they can be taught the difference between right and wrong, and programmed to act accordingly).

One roboticist who believes that robots can be taught to be moral is Shigeo Hirose. A robot that has been taught the difference between right and wrong would, says Hirose, act "correctly" in a situation fraught with ethical considerations. (He also believes that they could be "eternal," in the sense that their knowledge, backgrounds, and skills—their minds, in other words—could be downloaded to new robots.)

Some technologists, such as Hirose and Oracle Corporation's Larry Ellison, believe in the potential of AI and feel that the technology's possible benefits far outweigh any risks. Proponents point to possible uses in automation, weather forecasting, medical diagnostics, and surgery, among many other areas. As further evidence of the possibilities, some note the potential for AI-enhanced devices to be used in situations where it would be dangerous to send a human: caves, underwater caverns, bomb location and disposal, and many others.

Not everyone agrees that AI's benefits outweigh its risks, though. Physicist Stephen Hawking worried that, while AI might be "the biggest event in human history, . . . it might also be the last, unless we learn how to avoid the risks." Bill Gates has said that he's fine with AI until it gets *too* smart; he believes that the technology is both "promising and dangerous." Elon Musk, CEO of SpaceX and Tesla, has said that he felt that AI was ultimately an existential threat, a risk "vastly" more frightening than North Korea. Hawking, Musk, and Apple co-founder Steve Wozniak all signed off on a letter deeming AI potentially a threat to the human race, and "more dangerous than nuclear weapons."

The range of ethical issues associated with robotics and AI is large and vexing. (All ethical dilemmas are vexing, of course; this is why they're dilemmas.) We want robots and automation to help us, and they do—but they also put people out of work and disrupt entire industries. We want AI to help us complete tasks that are too onerous, dangerous, or time-consuming to handle without them, and they do—but we worry that if AI gets *too* smart, it could eventually outpace its human masters, and become so powerful that it—and robots using it—would no longer need humans.

Autonomous Vehicles

Over the last decade or so, self-driving vehicle technology has improved dramatically. In 2004, the Department of Defense offered a $1,000,000 cash prize for any self-driving car that could complete a 140-mile course across the Mojave Desert. Twenty-two cars entered the race; none finished. In fact, the most successful of the vehicles managed to complete only seven miles of the race. The following year, five cars finished. During a DOD-sponsored competition two years later, self-driving cars had to navigate an actual urban course, complete with traffic signals and other (nonautonomous) vehicles. Six cars successfully completed that race. After that, it was obvious that autonomous cars would eventually have a place on our highways and roads.

Some years after that last test, self-driving cars (and trucks) are a hot topic, and somewhere between 45 and 50 companies are working on autonomous vehicles, include big-name players such as Google/Alphabet, Tesla, Apple, Toyota, Ford, Audi, Nissan, and General Motors.

It's important to distinguish among types of autonomous vehicles, given that the levels of "autonomy" range from 0 (completely lacking in automation; today's "traditional" vehicles) to 5 (completely autonomous and generally lacking pedals and steering wheels).

Obviously, the vast majority of vehicles on the road today are level 0: the driver performs all driving tasks. Level 1 vehicles are controlled by the driver, but certain features may assist the driver in certain situations: parking, lane-changing, collision-avoidance. Many newer cars include one or more of these level 2 features. Some level 2 vehicles begin to approach true autonomy; steering and acceleration are autonomous, but the driver must monitor the vehicle at all times and be prepared to take control. Level 3 vehicles feature what is known as "conditional automation." The vehicle performs most actions; a driver is necessary, but is not required to monitor the environment, although he or she has to be ready to take control at all times. A level 4 vehicle is highly automated; under certain conditions, the vehicle is completely capable of performing all driving functions, although the driver may have the ability to take control of the vehicle. Level 5 vehicles are fully automated; the vehicle performs all tasks by itself under all conditions. The driver may have the ability to take control of the vehicle, but there may be little he can do other than stop, since the vehicle lacks pedals and a steering wheel.

There really are no level 3 (and certainly no level 4 or 5) vehicles on the market today. Tesla comes closest, but given the criteria above, a Tesla is really a level 2 vehicle, edging toward level 3.

Autonomous vehicles are an exciting development, but as with all new technologies, some ethical concerns arise. One of those is something we've already discussed when we examined robotics and AI: job loss. As with robotics and AI, the advent of truly autonomous vehicles will disrupt several industries. In this case, we can expect to see various levels of disruption— and consequent job loss—in the trucking and transportation industries, and we'll also likely see some radical changes for autoworkers themselves.

Realizing that the rise of autonomous vehicles will no doubt bring problems as well as benefits, the Union of Concerned Scientists in 2017 issued a policy brief aimed at maximizing the benefits of self-driving vehicles. The group noted that the technology "will create jobs for some and reduce employment opportunities for others, especially in the trucking and taxi industries." The group recommended that there be an effort to support employment transitions for affected individuals, that policy-makers should recognize and be prepared to deal with the economic impact of this new technology, and that new jobs created in the self-driving vehicle industry should be accessible to all, with a focus on increasing career opportunities for underrepresented populations.

One issue that may arise as the result of the deployment of autonomous vehicles is a possible increase in pollution. After all, once vehicles are truly automated, more people than ever may choose to ride in these cars, even people who may previously have carpooled, taken mass transit, walked, or ridden bicycles. The fact that large numbers of people may choose to hail a self-driving car could seriously disrupt mass transit, even as it adds those individual cars' pollution to the air. Then there's the problem of so-called **zombie cars**: autonomous vehicles without passengers that cruise the streets waiting to be hailed for a ride; assuming that those vehicles are not all-electric, those vehicles may create a significant amount of pollution.

Another issue has to do with "data sovereignty," the idea that any data created by you belongs to you. Yet, when your autonomous vehicle collects information from its many sensors, as it must in order to function, you really have very little control over that data. (Some analysts say that an autonomous car will generate about four terabytes of data—including location and video information—during a 90-minute drive.) It's processed in the vehicle, and much of it is then sent to servers where it is stored and analyzed by the manufacturer. You have no way of knowing whether the data is then sent to insurance companies or subpoenaed by law enforcement officials; not only are you unable to control who sees that information, you *yourself* have never seen most of it. You have ceded control of that information.

Autonomous vehicles will certainly bring about some positive changes, too. For one thing, there ought to be fewer accidents, since the computers driving these cars do not get tired or distracted, and since a swarm of autonomous vehicles will all watch out for one another and may even be in contact with one another.

We mentioned possible pollution resulting from the fact that more people may opt to take a car, but we also have to keep in mind that autonomous vehicles provide more options for disabled persons and for others who cannot drive, including those who are too young to drive but who need transportation to and from work or school. Some researchers estimate that more than 50 million people could directly benefit from self-driving vehicles.

Finally, just as the new vehicles will take away jobs from traditional industries, they will also add new jobs, and perhaps entire new industries. Fleets of autonomous cars will need maintenance and repair, programming, and design and analysis, and companies that build, maintain, or supply these vehicles will need project managers, assemblers, quality control personnel, and more.

Again, it's quite possible that the new vehicles will create more jobs than they eliminate; the issue will be whether people are prepared to take on those jobs. One of the ethical considerations attending the creation of these new industries is finding ways to ensure that people who are interested in new jobs are given the opportunity to qualify for those jobs.

Early in this review, we talked about the ethical issues inherent in the "trolley problem," and how those ethical concerns are just as valid—if not more so—when we consider autonomous vehicles. We said that there are, buried within the software that controls autonomous vehicles, certain ethical decisions that have been made by the designers and programmers. Some of those have to do with decisions about what the vehicle should do in the event of an unavoidable accident. The system must make what amounts to an ethical decision, a moral determination about which direction to turn to cause the "most acceptable" amount and type of damage.

This kind of decision-making hinges on what kind of moral perspective the designers brought to the problem; a utilitarian might opt for the "greater good" (i.e., the fewest people killed or injured), while a deontologist might try to determine what the "right" move might be. Of course, ethicists adhering to other schools of thought might have come up with some different decision and used different reasoning to reach that decision. The point is, a decision had to be made—and even *not* making a decision is, after all, a type of decision.

There are other ethical issues here, too. One has to do with accountability. If an accident did occur (and certainly, some must sooner or later occur), who is accountable for the accident? It can't be the human driver—unless he or she should have taken control and didn't. Perhaps it's the manufacturer? It could be the programmers, but which ones? This is very complex, sophisticated software, and many people no doubt worked on it; which programmer or team of programmers should bear the burden of responsibility?

One problem with considering this sort of accountability is that our legal systems are not set up to deal with such technology-driven questions. Germany's Ethics Commission on Automated Driving recently issued what is probably the first set of guidelines for what it called "self-driving computers" (i.e., autonomous vehicles). The commission's report notes that, with the advent of autonomous vehicles, the accountability that previously accrued to the individual shifts from the driver to the manufacturers and operators of the technology and to those who make policy and legal decisions. Thus, said the commission, the laws and the courts must move quickly so that they can fulfil their duties, among which are deciding issues of liability and accountability.

Finally, we come to perhaps the most subtle ethical issue associated with autonomous vehicles—and also with many other new technologies: loss of agency. In all of the autonomous car scenarios we've examined, the vehicle is making decisions. We want it to make those decisions; that's the point of an autonomous vehicle, after all: we expect the system to make good decisions, quickly and consistently. But by ceding our responsibility to make those decisions, we've eroded our agency, our ability to control ourselves and to make decisions that affect us. Instead, decisions that affect us are being made by an unknown and unnamed group of designers and programmers. Some ethicists say that this results in a devaluation of humanism, an ethical stance that puts human beings at the core of decisions and that emphasizes the agency of human beings—their ability to make the decisions that affect them.

Of course, if we want autonomous vehicles, this is the way it has to be. But ethicists worry about the cumulative effects of this erosion of agency spread over many years and many new technologies.

Social Justice Issues

Generally, **social justice** is defined as the equitable distribution of wealth, opportunity, and privilege. This is a somewhat abstract and debatable notion, given that people might disagree on, among other things, what "equitable" means in this context: Does it mean that everyone has a right to wealth? Or does it mean that everyone has a right to the opportunity to *earn* wealth? One thing that most ethicists agree on is that social justice means that people are not *prevented* from finding and taking advantage of opportunities to improve themselves and their lives, and that all people have access to the tools that would aid them in that pursuit.

NOTE: In the ongoing attempt to use technology to further social justice, one developer has created a Chrome extension called Uncover Harassers, which highlights the names of accused sexual harassers when they appear in your browser window—say, after a search of popular movie stars. However, the extension can flag only those *accused* of harassment, and these people are—in the United States—innocent until proven guilty. Some fear that the highlighting unfairly singles out people who have not yet—and may never—be found guilty of any crime.

It's an important issue, and technology plays a large part in how social justice is—or is not—attained by various populations, cultures, and nations. For some, the part that technology plays in social justice may be the most important ethical consideration of all. Mariette diChristina, former editor-in-chief of *Scientific American*, argues that failure to bring technology to all students may result in an inability to realize the potential innovations of our future. In other words, technology may be *the* social justice issue of what people are calling the "fourth industrial revolution."

The reality is that, if social justice is to be served, all people need access to technology. Technology (in the form of computers and the internet, certainly, but also including such basic technologies as electricity, tools, and telephones) is required in order to function in a global, interconnected society. There was a time, for example, when marketers trumpeted the sale of microcomputers as tools that would "give your student an advantage." A few years later, when so many households had computers, marketers shifted their sloganeering: now, they said that *not* having a computer would put the student at a *dis*advantage. Both slogans had some truth to them; the new language simply reflected a change in demographics and socioeconomics. Most people now had computers; if you did not have one, that may put you at a disadvantage in a classroom full of laptop-wielding students with instant access to information.

That gap between those who have access to technology and those who do not is still with us. There is a **digital divide** (also called a "technology gap"), exemplified (although not exclusively) by students who have computers and those who do not, or those who have high-speed internet and those who do not. Some studies show that students in low-income areas have less access to technology, and also that those in rural areas have less access than those in urban areas. Essentially, the rich and well educated are more likely, even today, to have more access to digital resources than the poor and poorly educated. The digital divide may not be as deep or as wide as it once was, but it still exists, even in so-called first-world nations; imagine the gap between those nations and undeveloped countries.

NOTE: There is still a digital divide in the United States. As of 2016, about 11% of the total population lacked any kind of internet access.

While technology has caused or exacerbated social justice issues, it has also helped to address such issues. One way it does that is by providing timely access to useful information, and the internet may be the most important tool we have for providing that access and for fostering social justice. Freeman Dyson, formerly of Cornell and the Institute for Advanced Study, points out that the internet can enable just about anyone to participate in the global economy, obtain an education, etc. He believes that ethics must help guide technology toward social justice.

In addition to the ethical issues associated with access—or lack of access—to the internet, other aspects of this technology also present ethical issues with which we must deal.

For example, your smartphone knows where you are. This is very handy when you're trying to find a campsite, a movie theater, or a restaurant. But that same data can be used by law enforcement or other government agencies to keep track of your location—if those agencies have access to the data.

Geotracking, as it is called, has become a big issue in both the fight against crime and the fight for data sovereignty. In some cases, law enforcement officials have been able to obtain geotracking data from cellular providers even without a warrant. That changed in June 2018 when the Supreme Court ruled 5-4 (in *Carpenter v. United States*) that, in most cases, the government needs a warrant in order to collect location data about cellphone companies' customers. But if the agency obtains a warrant, the technology that proved so helpful before may now prove your undoing.

One issue that we've already mentioned is the creation of filter bubbles or echo chambers that result when your social media feed adjusts itself programmatically to show you more subjects in which you've shown an interest. This is a convenient mechanism for ensuring that you see information in which you are interested, including posts from friends on which you've commented or posts you may have "liked" or "shared." But over time, your social media feed may evolve to the point where it shows you only information that accords with your beliefs. You are in an echo chamber—you see and hear information with which you already agree, and almost nothing with which you might not. How will you develop informed opinions if you're never exposed to alternative viewpoints? Your social media feed has become an ethical issue.

We've seen that technology can be a force for achieving social justice. The internet has democratized information and given millions the ability to compete in the world marketplace, while social networks keep people in touch no matter where they might be. At the same time, however, technology has created misinformation-spewing troll farms, "filter bubbles," and its relative absence in poor or rural areas has created social inequities. Freeman Dyson would say that it's up to us to see that technology is used in an ethical fashion, that we need to do what we can to ensure that the technology fosters, rather than impedes, social justice.

PROFESSIONAL ETHICS

Moral Obligations, Legal Liability, and Accountability of Corporations

If we're going to discuss professional ethics, we must first decide on our definition of a professional. It turns out that's not as simple as it sounds. Wearing a suit and going into an office every day does not make one a professional. We might agree that attorneys, doctors, IT staff, and teachers are all "professionals," but what is it about them that makes them professionals?

In determining what constitutes a professional, certain criteria are used. Among other things, a professional is one who: (1) has experience and knowledge certified by some certifying or licensing body and not possessed by a lay person; (2) exhibits a certain level of autonomy in one's day-to-day conduct of professional practice; and (3) is guided by a professional code of ethics that is used to guide, educate, and discipline practitioners.

A typical code of ethics for software engineers, for instance, is provided by the ACM/IEEE-CS Joint Task Force on Software Engineering Ethics and

Professional Practices. Among other things, the ACM code provides that (1) engineers shall act consistently with the public interest, (2) engineers shall maintain integrity and independence in their professional judgment, and (3) engineers shall participate in lifelong learning regarding the practice of their profession. The existence of a code of ethics means that there are certain standards that have been set and that must be followed by practitioners of that profession.

According to our three criteria, most IT experts are considered true professionals. Does that mean that they should consider broad ethical issues? Opinion is divided on that. The natural opinion for most of us would be that, since they are people living in a society, and since their work can impact many people in that society, of course they should consider broad ethical questions.

Some disagree, though. East Tennessee State University's Donald Gotterbarn, for example, has argued that computer scientists have no business considering broad moral questions unless they directly affect practitioners in their industry. Gotterbarn is not saying that professionals need not consider ethical issues at all, just that those considerations should be limited to issues relevant to the industry.

....

NOTE: Donald Gotterbarn is chair of the Association for Computing Machinery Committee on Professional Ethics and a professor emeritus at East Tennessee State University.

....

Not surprisingly, many of Gotterbarn's colleagues consider his views to be too narrow, especially in an age when computers are so ubiquitous and so much a part of just about all everyday social and business transactions. IT professionals, Gotterbarn's opponents argue, must bear some responsibility for the fact that their work impacts (for good or for ill) the ethical issues we've been discussing.

Responsibility—or accountability—is in fact a theme that is very much a part of the discussion of professional ethics.

In 1982, a Canadian company built a radiation treatment machine called the Therac-25. Due to errors in the design and manufacture, the machine killed three people and injured three more. Eventually, the malfunction was traced to multiple sources, including two software coding errors and a faulty switch. The major ethical issue here lay in deciding on accountability: There were dozens of people involved in the development of the machine: programmers, engineers, hardware designers, manufacturers, and others. Who is accountable?

To take an example we've already discussed in another context, in 2014, hackers broke into Apple's iCloud servers and stole (and then released) nude photos of celebrities. In that instance, who should be held responsible? The hackers themselves, surely. But what about Apple Corporation itself? Or the engineers and programmers who neglected to provide a secure storage environment? (In the end, the hackers were caught and charged, but no one at Apple was held responsible—at least, publicly.)

Helen Nissenbaum, whom we discussed earlier in the context of "contextual integrity," has pointed out that this is an example of what is called the **many hands problem**. When so many hands are involved in the design, building, programming, and configuration of systems such as the iCloud servers or Therac-25, it's difficult to determine accountability. We're used, says Nissenbaum, to discussing moral responsibility as if it were exclusionary: If we determine that A is responsible for some event, then that lets B and C off the hook. But in a "many hands" problem, accountability is diffuse; there may be several people—or several groups of people—who each bear some measure of responsibility. Since ethicists say that we need to ensure accountability for our actions, this causes an ethical dilemma.

Some feel that accountability—and ethical behavior in general—is more achievable when there is **transparency**; we behave better when we know we are being watched. If true, this means that corporations should ensure that their behavior is as transparent as possible.

This sounds simple, but the issue can be subtle. Take, for example, a search engine. There are certainly features to it that are transparent. We know how a search engine works—or we believe that we do. We enter search terms, the engine scours the web (actually it scours an index that is constantly being compiled and updated by the search engine company's web crawlers), and up pop matches that are based on those search terms. Morally, this is fairly transparent behavior.

But as ethicist and author Herman T. Tavani points out, there is more going on here. A search engine can be "morally controversial with respect to personal privacy." That is, the company behind the search engine stores your searches, correlates them with other users' searches, and sells that data to marketers. This is how search engines make money and why they can offer such a useful service at no charge. The fact that we may not realize that there is something going on behind the scenes makes that behavior opaque, rather than transparent. The behavior is thus ethically question-able, because the search engine's actions (really, the actions of the people behind the search engine) are not transparent.

> **NOTE:** Herman T. Tavani is the author of *Ethics and Technology* and the winner of the 2019 Weizenbaum Award, given every two years by the International Society for Ethics and Information Technology (INSEIT).

Moral Responsibilities of IT Professionals

IT professionals have many job responsibilities, of course, but they also have ethical responsibilities—to their employers, to fellow employees, and to the public. Note that **responsibility** and **liability** are two different things; the former is an ethical or moral consideration, the latter is a legal concept; a person might be responsible for an IT issue, but the company would most likely be held liable.

As we noted earlier, professionals follow a code of ethics; that's part of what makes them professionals. In the case of IT workers, one of those applicable codes of ethics is that published by the Association of Computing Machinery (ACM). The code requires, among other things, that IT pros: (1) support the public good; (2) provide full disclosure of all system capabilities, limitations, and potential problems; and (3) understand the responsibilities associated with the collection of personal information.

> **NOTE:** The ACM is quite old, having been established in 1947. It is the world's largest educational computing society, with nearly 100,000 members.

There are other IT-related codes of conduct, of course. The "Ten Commandments of Computer Ethics," created in 1992 by members of the Computer Ethics Institute (CEI), are widely known and often quoted among technology ethicists and practitioners of the IT professions. Among those commandments are the following: (1) Thou shalt think about the social consequences of the program you are writing; (2) Absent permission, thou shalt not copy or use proprietary software; and (3) Thou shalt not use a computer to harm other people.

Not everyone agrees with the commandments, by the way—or at least, not all of them. CEI's Ben Fairweather picks apart many of the commandments, noting, for example, that the commandment prescribing that professionals must "think about the social consequences" of their programs is much too simplistic. He feels that mere thought is pointless. Practitioners, he says, must *act* upon those thoughts. Fairweather is not at all sure that just adhering to the commandments is enough. He also notes that some commandments seem fairly trivial, but the listing seems to imply that all of them are equally important.

Keep in mind, by the way, that most codes stipulate that intent does not preclude responsibility. If you intend to follow the precepts of a particular code of ethics, but accidentally breach one of those requirements (say you forget to encrypt personal data and left it exposed to a potential hack), that does not excuse you. If you intend to be a professional, then you are responsible for following the precepts laid out in your professional code—it doesn't matter that you intended to follow the code but failed; you're still responsible for any negative outcomes, and your intent does not excuse those failures.

Most IT-related professional codes understandably require loyalty to one's employer. Your employer is, after all, paying your salary. However, this cannot be an *unquestionable* obligation; if it were, there could be many times when it would conflict with one of the other precepts of the code. For instance, there may very well come a time when you have to put your commitment to the public good above loyalty to your employer. When that happens, we have entered the realm of "whistleblowing."

Whistleblowers are those who expose, often at great risk to themselves, information or activity within an organization that they feel is illegal or unethical. A whistleblower is, by definition, someone who is inherently disloyal to someone, and who has chosen to betray someone—often an employer. Often, a whistleblower finds him- or herself in the position of breaking the law by making public information or behavior that was intended to be secret.

Most ethicists say that there are times when an employee is permitted to blow the whistle on an employer. And there are also times, say ethicists, when one is obligated to do so.

University of Kansas professor and business ethicist Richard T. De George has created a framework designed to determine when an employee is *permitted* to "blow the whistle" on a company practice and when the employee is *obligated* to do so. According to De George, an IT employee is permitted to blow the whistle when the following conditions exist:

1. The harm that will be done by the product [or company action] to the public is serious and considerable.
2. The engineer (or employee) has made his or her concerns known to superiors.

3. The engineer (or employee) has received no satisfaction from immediate supervisors and has exhausted the channels available within the company, including going to the board of directors.

> **NOTE:** Richard T. De George is Distinguished Professor of Philosophy and of Russian and East European Studies, and Co-Director of the International Center for Ethics in Business at the University of Kansas.

At this stage, says De George, the employee has moral authority to blow the whistle. De George maintains that the employee has the obligation, the moral duty, to blow the whistle if the following two additional conditions are met:

1. The engineer has accessible and documented evidence that would convince a reasonable, impartial observer that his or her concern for public safety is correct and the company product or action is likely to cause serious and considerable public harm.
2. There is strong evidence that making the information public will in fact prevent the threatened serious harm.

Notable whistleblowers throughout history include police officer Frank Serpico, Karen Silkwood, and the FBI's Mark Felt (a.k.a. deep throat). The most famous whistleblower in recent years has been Edward Snowden. Snowden was a National Security Agency (NSA) IT contractor who leaked NSA information in 2013. The leaked material detailed secret global surveillance programs, many run by the NSA. The leaks caused an uproar and serious arguments about ethics, mostly centered on whether his breaking the law was morally justifiable. There was little argument about whether he had actually broken the law; the question was—and remains—was he permitted to do so? Was he obligated to do so?

> **NOTE:** Mark Felt, the number two man at the FBI during the tumultuous 1970s, did not admit to being "deep throat" until a 2005 interview with *Vanity Fair*, during which the 91-year-old Felt admitted feeding information to *Washington Post* reporters Bob Woodward and Carl Bernstein during the Watergate crisis.

We can apply De George's criteria to Snowden's actions, in which case we're likely to find that Snowden met most of the criteria: The issues at hand could certainly do harm to the public, he did report his issues to his supervisors, and he had "accessible, documented evidence" that could have convinced a reasonable observer that his suspicions were correct.

There is one criterion that we can't be sure of, however. We have no way of knowing for sure that Snowden "exhausted the internal procedures, including contacting the board of directors" (or the NSA's equivalent to a board of directors).

The uproar continues today. Snowden released the information to several publications, including Julian Assange's *WikiLeaks*. US authorities are still trying to extradite Assange on various charges, some of which stem from Snowden's whistleblowing. As of this printing, Assange is in a British prison awaiting possible extradition, and Snowden was granted permanent residency in Russia.

Because whistleblowing can apply to very specific internal issues and also to broader ethical impacts, the Snowden affair brings up the issue of **microethics** versus **macroethics**. The former has to do with individuals and with internal relations in the individual's profession. The latter is more concerned with collective social responsibility and with broader societal decisions about technology.

As an example, consider a company meeting that includes a discussion about programmers complying with safe programming practices. Absent any other qualifying information, this is a microethical concern: people within the company are discussing the issue and how best to ensure that certain practices are followed by the company's programmers. Contrast that scenario with a discussion about the impact of social media on social justice: this latter discussion is much more general and more broadly applicable than the other scenario. This is a macroethical topic.

Someone going to work in an IT environment soon after college or certification may not have given much thought to ethical issues as they impact, or are impacted by, the IT profession. But the reality is that few professions—few jobs, in fact—are completely divorced from possible ethical concerns; the question of morality almost always comes with the territory.

The Role of the Press

Ethics has more than just "a place" in the practice of journalism; it is the foundation of journalism—at least, as practiced in a free country.

The primary goal of a free press is **objectivity**. News must be reported factually, with no slant, and must not be confused with opinion and analysis. There is certainly a place for opinion and analysis in a free press, and there always has been. However, professional ethics require that those be clearly labeled, and that the news outlet must not attempt to pass them off as "news."

Unfortunately, this primary journalistic goal occasionally conflicts with an even more basic goal: the need to make money. Whatever the mechanics of publication—newspaper, radio, television, website, blog, etc.—publishing costs money. If the newspaper or magazine were to lose sight of that, then the publication would soon cease to exist, and thus forfeit its ability to perform its primary duty of informing the public; a newspaper that goes out of business is no longer in a position to inform. In a free society, journalists are seen as stewards of the citizenry and of their rights; the First Amendment guarantees freedom of expression, thus guaranteeing citizens their right to free speech, which is partly attained through their free press. If the company behind the news outlet operated in such a fashion that it had to cease publication, it would have ceded its obligation to act as a steward of those rights.

NOTE: At least in the United States, newspapers are dying, with both ad revenues and circulation numbers shrinking. In 2014, there were 126 fewer daily papers than in 2004. In the years since, many print newspapers publishers have gone to a hybrid online/print model, offered online-only editions, or disappeared altogether.

The code of ethics of the American Society of News Editors states that journalism "demands of its practitioners not only industry and knowledge but also the pursuit of a standard of integrity proportionate to the journalist's singular obligation." Integrity is a cornerstone of ethics and ethical behavior, and it is supposed to inform every aspect of that obligation.

Part of that integrity comes from the ability to acquire information from sources without giving up the names of those sources. In most states, a "shield law" of some sort protects reporters, shielding them from being forced to reveal sources, and in many states, this privilege has been recognized by the court. The law does not always shield reporters, however, and many have been forced to give up their sources or have gone to jail to protect those sources. Still, 49 states plus the District of Columbia offer some form of protection for reporters who wish not to reveal their sources. Wyoming is the only state that does not offer any protection.

But journalism is changing, and much of that change is due to innovations in technology. In previous eras, publishers used newspapers and magazines (and then later, TV and radio) as platforms for delivering the news, but we now have a collection of what Harvard Law School professor Yochai Benkler calls, "the new, networked media." To the mix of traditional journalism outlets, we've recently added websites, blogs, social media, YouTube, and more. Millennials, especially, get much of their news from social networking sites such as Facebook. Only some 24% of millennials still watch television, and about 38% of all adults get most or all of their news online. Digital media wields much of the power that used to belong to traditional media.

> **NOTE:** Yochai Benkler is the Berkman Professor of Entrepreneurial Legal Studies at Harvard Law School and a faculty co-director of the Berkman Klein Center for Internet & Society at Harvard University. His most recent book is *Network Propaganda: Manipulation, Disinformation, and Radicalization in American Politics.*

Dr. Benkler does not necessarily view the emergence of new media as problematic, though it's definitely a shift that is disrupting both viewing habits and the business models of existing media purveyors. He believes that traditional media and the "new, networked media" have come together in a "new media environment."

The rise of the new media does bring up several questions related to the ethical practice of journalism. For instance, can a blogger be considered a journalist? In the view of most journalism-related codes of ethics, not usually. Journalists deal in facts, which they acquire through research and interviews with subject matter experts and eyewitnesses. Bloggers tend to deal mostly with opinions and analysis. (Not that this is entirely a bad thing; many of these opinions and analyses are thoughtful, articulate, and well-reasoned.) Rather than "journalist," the term being used—sometimes derisively—to describe bloggers, vloggers, and web-based pundits is "media influencer."

Many of the "news" bloggers and websites lack a commitment to objectivity and professionalism; this affects their credibility, though it doesn't seem to affect their appeal. (It may be that the same could be said about some traditional news outlets.) Some new media outlets, though, have begun to acquire reputations for objectivity and accuracy, often in niche areas; some cybersecurity blogs, for instance, are trusted primary sources of information in that area. It's possible that we will end up with a solid collection of new media outlets that we've learned to trust—and which have earned that trust.

Given the emphasis on ethics in journalism, it's not surprising that there are several journalistic codes of ethics. As mentioned earlier, the code of ethics of the American Society of News Editors states that journalism "demands of its practitioners not only industry and knowledge but also the pursuit of a standard of integrity proportionate to the journalist's singular obligation." There are also codes of ethics promulgated by the Society of Professional Journalists, the Ethical Journalism Network, and others.

And yet, there are no *statutory* codes; that is, there are no laws that govern how a journalist must act. There's a good reason for that: If a reporter were subject to statutory laws (especially federal laws) that governed his or her behavior, there might be many situations in which the reporter would be faced with the choice of acting ethically or acting legally. (This already occurs on occasion, even absent such statutes.)

Social Media: Positive Reinforcement and Dissemination of Unfounded Information

As we've noted, the problem with democratizing information is that when we do that, we also democratize *mis*information. Anyone can publish on the internet, because there are no real barriers to entry. In many ways this is a positive development, but it also means that very little is done to police the new media publishers; the fact that something is published on the internet does not mean that is true, accurate, or that the published snippet tells the whole story.

Most of us would like to hold social media to the same standards as other media: newspapers, radio, television, etc. But unlike news in a newspaper or news broadcast, the content on social media sites is almost all user-created. It may in fact be fair, objective, and factual, in keeping with the ethical codes to which we hold more traditional news organizations, but it may not. What we would call the "publishers," the platform providers, generally don't create the content, so the law (in the United States, Section 230 of the Communication Decency Act) says that they cannot be held responsible for it.

So, who *is* responsible for that content?

We might decide that the platform providers are responsible for policing the platform's user-generated content, seeking to ensure that if it is not factual and objective, it at least does not attempt to incite violence or hatred, and that it does not actively and purposefully spread misinformation. Of course, forcing platform providers to comply has proven difficult, given that they're not legally liable and that such policing costs money and may alienate media influencers whose accounts generate revenue for both the account holder and the social network.

> **NOTE:** In 2010, there were fewer than 1 billion social media users. In 2021, there are expected to be more than 3 billion.

Some countries, however, have taken steps to ensure that content gets policed and vetted. Germany, for instance, recently passed stringent hate-speech laws, and said that Facebook must ensure that its content abides by those laws, even if that meant that the social network had to spend money hiring German-speaking moderators. As a result, in spite of having previously argued that it was impossible to do so, the company hired a huge number of moderators and deployed new features designed to catch and reduce hate speech.

Facebook recently shut down some 3 billion abusive accounts, most of which were fake and many of which were run by bots. Even afterward, though, it is estimated that about 5% of Facebook's accounts are fake. That's a fairly small percentage, but there are 2 billion accounts, so that means that about 100 million of them are fake.

Generally, though, media analysts say that the law has not kept pace with the legal issues generated by the new media. Obviously, this causes legal problems, but it also creates ethical dilemmas.

For example, suppose Louis stays home from work one day claiming illness, but his Facebook posts show him at a party that evening. His supervisor, having seen Louis' posts, reprimands and demotes him for lying about his illness. Aside from the potential legal issues, we're left with an ethical question: Is it right for social media status updates be used as evidence in such cases (or in any case)? Can an employer use someone's social network posts to make or support judgements about the worker? We can argue about the answer(s) to that question (and about the worker's questionable work ethic), but the root ethical issue here is privacy: Is it right that Louis's actions can be viewed and acted upon? Is it appropriate for that portion of his life to be visible to his employer? The *legal* issue has to do with whether an employee can have his employment affected by what he does when he's away from work, but the ethical issue—though related to the legal one—has more to do with how much of Louis' life is private and how much is not.

NOTE: You can be—and several people have been—fired for Facebook posts. A woman who worked for the Iowa Department of Public Safety was fired after posting about her fear that she might be attacked by black people. In 2015, a Chicago-area zoo employee was fired after a rude post about white people. In 2018, an employee of Hilton Grand Vacations was fired after a racist post about Florida State University coach Willie Taggart. And a Florida school board member declined to run for a third term after pushback as a result of posting harsh comments about women who were raped and implying that they deserved it.

We know that—perhaps thanks partly to the disinhibition effect we discussed earlier—people lie on social media, and they may or may not be held accountable for those lies. But what happens when a law enforcement officer lies on social media? When Sondra Prince was arrested on drug charges in 2010, the DEA seized her mobile phone, used it to set up a fake Facebook page under her name and, using photos of Prince, entrapped several of her Facebook "friends" who thought they were communicating with Prince. (Prince eventually sued the DEA and the agency settled out of court for a bit more than $130,000.)

People have always lied, but now, thanks to the internet, they can lie much more effectively and to many, many more people—millions of people, in fact.

The lies are getting harder to uncover, as we've seen with the recent introduction of deepfakes, fake videos and audios of people seemingly doing and saying things they never said or did in real life. Recall that deepfakes are created using artificial intelligence and sophisticated editing techniques, and then spread via social media. They're so well done that they can be very difficult to tell from the real thing.

The thing about deepfakes is that they bring into play what is called the **liar's dividend**. People who really *did* say or do something can simply point to the evidence and call it a lie, whether a deepfake or something else. After all, whom should people trust? What's true, when seeing might no longer be believing? Some researchers have said that the very *idea* of truth may decay as a result of deepfakes. Even after retractions are printed and someone has determined what's real and what's not, the original story—the deepfake—will be the one that's remembered.

There's also a powerful psychological component to our use of social media. Sometimes that component ties into a marketer's appeal. For instance, marketers will use the word "free" as a way to get users to click and engage with an ad. Businesses wish to encourage a social media conversation, partly to generate word-of-mouth, so they'll attempt the "freebie" gambit: "Click here and follow to win a [insert prize here] for FREE!" We love free stuff, and it's worth giving away something for free (if, in the end, they really are doing so) if they can get people to talk about their product or their company. Word-of-mouth is what sells products, and there's no place better to build word-of-mouth than on social media.

Even without free goodies, though, posts and responses to posts act as positive reinforcement, and this has some ethicists, psychologists, and sociologists worried.

When we receive a message, we perceive that as a positive, especially if the message says something good about us or about something we posted earlier. But *any* response that's not an actual attack tends to generate positive feelings. That repeated reinforcement can boost self-confidence, though that self-confidence may be unwarranted; more importantly, it may be the key to what many believe are addictive behaviors associated with social media.

Excessive checking of devices is one of those behaviors. Psychologists say that the fear of missing out (known as FOMO) may account for some of the addictive behavior we see exhibited by people, young and old, who cannot bear to be unconnected for any length of time. Since just about any post or message is seen as positive reinforcement, the absence of that positive reinforcement can be almost physically painful. That is the very definition of an addiction.

NOTE: FOMO is a real thing, and psychologists have been studying it to help determine its psychological basis. Researchers at Carleton and McGill University examined the social and psychological basis of FOMO, and concluded that FOMO was greatest at the end of the day and near the end of the week. It was also associated with fatigue, stress, and sleep problems.

Net Neutrality

The arguments for and against so-called net neutrality have been going strong since approximately 2014. In fact, in late 2014, a global coalition from 19 countries launched an initiative to encourage "a basic, collaborative, and universal definition" of net neutrality.

That definition of **net neutrality** is relatively simple, though arguments about it have become complex and politically charged. The internet has always been "neutral" in the sense that no one content stream has been favored over another. If you stream YouTube and Netflix videos all day long (and thus consume a great deal of bandwidth), you pay the same for your access as the person who merely checks email and occasionally surfs the web. And when he or she does surf the web, one type of website costs the same as any other website, in terms of what you're paying to access the site. (The cost of the content itself may differ from one provider to another—an eBook may cost more than, say, music you download from Apple or Google—but the *bandwidth* you're using costs the same regardless.) This has been in keeping with a broad contingent of users who believe that all content should be accessible to all, and that providers should not be able to charge different rates for different types of content.

That neutrality was formalized and codified in rules adopted by the FCC in 2016. However, those rules were officially reversed ("disapproved" was the term used) in June 2018, partly due to lobbying by FCC head Ajit Pai, who argued that the government should not be in charge of what amounts to an information utility.

Large content providers such as Google, Amazon, and Netflix tend to be in favor of net neutrality, at least in part because a lack of neutrality—that is, the existence of "tiered" service levels—would negatively affect their customer base.

Large service providers, such as Verizon and AT&T, have tended to be against net neutrality. They argue that someone who consumes a great deal of bandwidth—or critical data feeds—should not pay the same amount as someone who consumes very little bandwidth.

In what some had likened to a preview of the repeal of net neutrality, Netflix—whose customers had naturally been consuming huge amounts of bandwidth—made a deal with Comcast and Verizon in 2014 to allow

Netflix to stream video unimpeded to Comcast and Verizon customers. Under this "paid peering" deal, Netflix could connect directly to Comcast's network instead of going through intermediaries. The fear, though, was that if Netflix was paying more for that access, the company would simply pass those costs on to the consumer, in effect creating a tiered internet.

There are a number of well-reasoned arguments both for and against net neutrality.

One argument used by proponents of net neutrality has to do with innovation and startups. Proponents say that small companies will be squeezed out because they don't have the buying power to compete with the big service providers.

Also, many US cities were (and are) planning to implement "smart city" projects that could include intelligent building, transportation, and energy systems. These systems would include motion and flow sensors, video cameras, and temperature and noise monitors, all of which would send data over the internet. The fear is that, if the internet is suddenly not a "level playing field," rising costs could derail these plans.

One (somewhat unusual) argument against the repeal of net neutrality was that it would become a "political football," with the rules returning if the Democrats take power. Some argued that the whole argument is political, with net neutrality being favored by most Democrats and its repeal favored by most Republicans. They reason that the problem really hinges on political instability, and that the argument will simply go back and forth as each party takes control over the years, so why repeal the existing neutrality in the first place?

Opponents of net neutrality, on the other hand, marshal a number of (mostly business-oriented) arguments seeking to show that net neutrality is inherently unfair, not only to some consumers, but also to the companies that must pay for the infrastructure on which the internet runs.

One such argument is that a so-called tiered internet will enable ISPs to prioritize internet traffic, especially IoT traffic. This means that communications from medical devices or autonomous vehicles, for example, could be put in the fast lane. This could literally be a matter of life and death, given that the data being transferred in such cases might be life-saving.

Opponents of net neutrality further argue that some internet services simply cost providers more and use up more of their bandwidth; for example, a user who occasionally surfs the web and checks email does not use nearly the bandwidth as someone who streams movies all night. The providers argue that the latter person should pay more for his or her internet service. If you use up more of the provider's bandwidth, goes the opponents' argument, you should pay more than someone who uses less.

Finally, opponents of net neutrality say that without it, the internet is, in effect, controlled by the government, and they feel that if the internet were controlled by private interests, it would be in better hands.

> **NOTE:** Some feel that the internet should not be controlled by the government simply because they don't trust the government to do a good job. According to the Pew Research Center, in the United States, trust in the government has dropped from about 75% during the Eisenhower years to less than 20% during the late-Obama/early-Trump eras.

Most users favor net neutrality, but then (goes the opponents' argument) they're not the ones charged with building out and maintaining the infrastructure on which it runs. Nor do they pay for the research that leads to new infrastructure, developments, or products. In other words, they have little invested in the internet, but they reap all the benefits.

It's possible that the net neutrality laws will be reversed—or "un-disapproved," if you prefer. The Save the Internet Act was introduced and passed by the US House of Representatives in 2019. (It is definitely a partisan issue; only one Republican voted in favor of the act.) It seeks to restore net neutrality. However, as of 2020, the act was still awaiting Senate approval.

NEW OR OLD? CREATED OR EXACERBATED?

Ethical issues are all about tensions: tensions between privacy and security, between citizens' rights and law enforcement agencies' need to protect those citizens, between one's right to free speech and the public's right to be free of hateful or violence-inciting speech, between our freedom of choice and others' right to remain unaffected by our choices. Finding ways to resolve those tensions is what ethicists seek to do, and people who wish to "do the right thing" seek such resolutions every day.

In this chapter review, we've seen several examples of unethical behavior by scammers, over-zealous marketers, hackers, and more, and we've talked about several ethical issues related to technology. One key question to keep in mind about ethics in technology is one that ethicists continue to debate: Are these *new* issues, or simply *old* ones given new life by technology? Some feel that technology has created new and unique ethical issues, while others believe that there *are* no new ethical issues. Technology may have exacerbated old issues, they say, but it did not create new ones.

Whichever side of that argument you take (and the answer may not truly matter a whole lot—the issues are present, whether or not they're new), this review should have given you enough background to realize that those ethical questions—new or old—do exist. More to the point, the questions and ethical dilemmas are *important*, if for no other reason than the fact that these new technologies are ubiquitous and far-reaching. Like it or not, we will be (in fact, *are being*) impacted both by the technologies we've discussed and the ethical considerations that have emerged as a result of those technologies.

SUMMING IT UP

- **Cyberethics** is the study of moral, legal, and social issues that are impacted or caused by technology.
- **Utilitarian** ethics is the school of thought that maintains that the *consequences* are what's important. From the utilitarian perspective of a cost-benefit analysis, does an action harm more people than it helps, or help more people than it harms?
- **Deontological** or "normative" ethics maintains that it's what's *right* that matters most, that there is always a right thing to do and a wrong thing to do, and one should do what is right.
- **Technology** exacerbates existing ethical issues; some ethicists believe that it has created completely *new* issues.
- **Privacy** is a key issue in technology, and it comes into play when we're discussing hackers, government access to data, or users who share or overshare data.
- **Cookies** are small text files saved on your hard drive by a website. **First-party cookies** are useful for website navigation; these "session cookies" are erased when you leave the site. **Persistent cookies** remain on your hard drive and are often used to help you log in when you revisit the site. **Third-party cookies** can be used by advertisers or marketers to track your browsing and buying behavior. **"Zombie cookies"** reappear even after you've erased them.
- Helen Nissenbaum has discussed what she calls the **contextual integrity** issue, noting that we're comfortable sharing data when we can select—and control—the context.

- **Doxing** (or doxxing) is collecting and publishing someone's personal information, which can lead to real-life stalking or can affect someone's work or personal life.
- In **swatting**, an attacker will phone a serious issue requiring a police presence using the address of a target who may not know he or she is the subject of an attack. The goal is to get the police (perhaps even a SWAT team) to show up, armed and ready to force entry to the target's home or office. Swatting has resulted in at least one death.
- **Social engineering** is a form of attack that relies mainly on deceit and trickery. **Phishing** and **catfishing** are forms of social engineering, as is someone showing up at your office pretending to be a contractor or serviceperson.
- The **disinhibition effect** occurs when people attack using the anonymity of the internet as a shield; it greatly reduces the fear that would ordinarily inhibit us from attacking another person or group.
- Section 230 of the 1996 **Communications Decency Act** specifically shields platform providers (Facebook, etc.) from liability for what users post on their platforms.
- Social media can be addictive. When our computer, phone, or tablet chimes, that is a form of positive reinforcement, and we eventually get to the point where we need that almost-constant positive reinforcement.
- On social networks, we often find ourselves in a **social media bubble** in which we hear only the opinions of people who agree with us and little or nothing from those with whom we might disagree.
- A **Stingray** is a device that can mimic a cell tower, forcing all communications to flow through the device, where they can be intercepted.
- **Dark phones** are those that are encrypted or otherwise protected from entry by anyone other than the owner, including law enforcement agencies.
- **Big data** refers not only to the size of the data collection efforts (massive), but also to the data's structure—or lack of structure. Big data collects huge amounts of possibly unrelated and unstructured data (generally, datasets that are too large or complex to be processed by traditional means), and then uses massive computing power (and sometimes artificial intelligence) to make sense of that information.
- **Agency** is a psychology term describing the idea that we are in control of our own actions, thoughts, and behaviors. When advertisers or others attempt to influence us, we lose agency.
- Most browsers implemented **Do Not Track (DNT)** requests in the mid-2000s, but these are voluntary and generally ineffective since so few honor those requests.

- There are no federal laws regulating data breaches and data breach reporting, but every state has its own laws. The first and one of the most stringent was California's 2018 California Consumer Privacy Act (CCPA).
- The **Critical Infrastructure Information Act (CIIA)**, passed in 2002, required that infrastructure providers (those whose companies or agencies provide gas, electric, water, and other such utilities) communicate with government personnel as a way to reduce the country's vulnerability to terrorism.
- Section 203 of the PATRIOT Act empowers law enforcement officials to share criminal investigative information that contains foreign intelligence or counterintelligence with intelligence and national-security personnel.
- In 2014, hackers breached Apple Corporation's iCloud **cloud storage service** and stole (and then distributed) nude photos, many of them belonging to celebrities, including model Kate Upton and actress Jennifer Lawrence. The hack became known as **celebgate**.
- In 2013, giant retailer Target Corporation was the victim of a data breach that affected millions of its customers. The company initially reported that 40 million customers had been affected, but then had to revise that figure upward to 110 million.
- **Hacktivists** are hackers for a cause. They aim to disrupt the infrastructure of their perceived enemies. The most well-known hacktivist group is Anonymous.
- **Counter-hacking** (or "hacking back") is illegal, violating the (1984) Computer Fraud and Abuse Act, which outlaws almost any form of unauthorized access or access with ill intent.
- **Information warfare** is the weaponized use of information (or misinformation) to create a strategic or tactical advantage.
- A **bot** (short for "web robot") is software that runs on a social network that can be used to automatically tweet or retweet, like or unlike a post, and follow or unfollow a person.
- UK firm Cambridge Analytica was accused of utilizing "dirty tricks" in Donald Trump's 2016 Presidential campaign. Further, the company was accused of collaborating with Russian agents during the incident.
- The **just war hypothesis**, say tech ethicists, fails when applied to technology, because the risks for an "attacker" using information as a weapon are much less than for a traditional attacker.
- A **denial of service (DoS)** attack is among the simplest of cyberattacks: a computer simply sends, and keeps sending, requests to a server or group of servers until the servers are so overwhelmed that they cannot function and cannot respond to "real" requests. A **distributed denial of service (DDoS)** attack is one that enlists the help of many bot-controlled devices or computers to launch the attack.

- Social media platforms (and ISPs) are private companies and are free to censor if they choose to do so.
- Hate speech is on the rise: according to the Southern Poverty Law Center, between 1995 and 2000, the number of websites featuring hate speech had increased about 250%.
- In November 2018, the government of France passed an "anti-fake news" law that authorizes the immediate removal of "fake news" during election campaigns.
- The ethical dilemma over free speech on the internet can be summed up as the tension between citizens' rights to champion their viewpoints and society's right to be protected from what they find abhorrent views—especially views that might become dangerous rhetoric that could incite violence.
- Nowhere does the US Constitution explicitly guarantee a right to privacy, though some say it is implied in the Fourth and Fourteenth Amendments.
- The (2003) **Controlling the Assault of Non-Solicited Pornography and Marketing Act (CAN-SPAM Act)** governs the sending of unsolicited commercial emails and prohibits deceptive subject lines in emails.
- The (2003) **Fair and Accurate Credit Transactions Act (FACTA**, an amendment to the Fair Credit Reporting Act) requires financial institutions and creditors to maintain written identity theft prevention programs in an effort to guard against identity theft.
- The (1984) **Computer Fraud and Abuse Act (CFAA)** outlaws various types of online fraud, including trafficking in passwords, and prohibits even *unintentional* damage if "reckless disregard" is shown.
- **Intellectual property** is a category of property that includes intangible creations, such as trademarks, patents, or designs, among others. IP laws exist to protect the creators of such properties so that they can realize an economic benefit for their efforts.
- **Public domain** works can be used by anyone for any purpose. Works created prior to the existence of copyright law are in the public domain, as are works whose copyright has expired or whose creator has purposely placed them in the public domain.
- The **fair use clause** of the copyright law clause notes that teachers, writers, critics, and others can use portions of copyrighted works in certain circumstances. One of those circumstances is in education, and another is in critical or analytical works.
- **Open-source** software can be free or fee-based, and it includes the source code so that users are able to modify the software and distribute the modified versions of that software.

- The 1998 **Digital Millennium Copyright Act (DMCA)** criminalized technologies that attempt to circumvent various forms of digital rights management (DRM), also known as copy protection. One important impact of the DMCA was that it shielded ISPs and other intermediaries from both direct and indirect liabilities, meaning that they could not be held responsible for what was published by those using their services.
- The ethical issue relating to **copyright infringement** arises from the fact that, although it is illegal (and ethically suspect) to make use of someone else's intellectual property, modern technology makes it very simple to do.
- Intelligence and law enforcement agencies often (and often for good reason) seek what is known as **lawful access** to protected or encrypted data on your phone or other device. This is related to the "dark phone" issue noted above.
- The **All Writs Act of 1789** authorizes courts to compel third parties to assist in the execution of a court order, and in the 2015 case against Apple, Inc., the FBI argued that the law applied there. The FBI was attempting to access encrypted information on a terrorist suspect's phone.
- **Ransomware** is a special kind of cyberextortion that involves encrypting a victim's files and demanding a ransom to decrypt the files.
- **James Moor** believes that cyberethics issues are unique because they've been created by unique technology. A computer, he says, is "logically malleable"; rather than being created for a single purpose, it can be instructed to do many things. Therefore, says Moor, it creates "new possibilities for human action."
- Ethicist **Walter Maner** feels that, if nothing else, technology-related ethical issues must be viewed as unique simply because the technology is uniquely fast and uniquely complex.
- **Genetically modified organisms (GMO)** are seeds or plants that have been genetically modified such that they gain some advantageous trait: perhaps they're hardier, need less water, grow larger, or are more resistant to pesticides, among other possible advantages.
- One ethical (and legal) issue that has arisen is the question of who has rights to blood and tissue samples taken from you during a medical procedure done in a US facility. You might think that those automatically belong to you, but you would be incorrect, according to several court decisions.
- **Induced pluripotent stem (iPS) cells** are taken from adult donors and, like stem cells, can become any type of cell in the body. They cannot replace stem cells in every respect and for all types of research.
- Few **Internet of Things (IoT)** devices are well-secured; thus, the frequent reports of hacked baby monitors, routers, automated building systems, and (somewhat ironically) security cameras.

- The big question with IoT devices has to do with "data sovereignty." What happens with that data? Who owns it? For what purposes can it be used?
- Alexa may be the most ubiquitous example of IoT technology in the home. More than 100 million Alexa devices have been sold, and recordings made by Alexa are stored on Amazon's servers.
- The fear of new technology affecting jobs is not new. It goes back to the Luddites and before. The **Luddites** were English textile workers who had lost their jobs as new machinery took over the industry.
- Mid-level white-collar workers with intermediate skills are finding that much of their work is now—or will soon be—performed by computer programs.
- Some say that 47% of jobs will someday be automated, and that 30% will *soon* be automated.
- A **deepfake** is made by using **artificial intelligence (AI)** to combine or superimpose images or videos to create fake videos of people doing or saying things they never actually did or said.
- The thought of a weapon that can decide on its own when (and what) to attack frightens many ethicists and more than a few scientists. A 2015 open letter signed by 25,000 AI professionals requested that research on autonomous weapons be banned.
- Physicist **Stephen Hawking** worried that, while AI might be "the biggest event in human history, . . . it might also be the last, unless we learn how to avoid the risks."
- **Elon Musk**, CEO of SpaceX and Tesla, has said that he felt that AI was ultimately an existential threat, a risk "vastly" more frightening than North Korea.
- **Zombie cars** are autonomous vehicles without passengers that cruise the streets waiting to be hailed for a ride; these may cause pollution.
- **Data sovereignty** is the idea that any data created by you belongs to you. Yet, when your autonomous vehicle collects information from its many sensors, as it must in order to function, you really have very little control over that data.
- **Social justice** is defined as the equitable distribution of wealth, opportunity, and privilege.
- There is a **digital divide** (also called a "technology gap"), largely exemplified by students who have computers and those who do not, or those who have high-speed internet and those who do not.
- Some feel that the internet may be the single most important tool for fostering social justice, as it can enable anyone to participate in the global economy or obtain an education.

- Most define a **professional** as one who (1) has experience and knowledge certified by some certifying or licensing body and not possessed by a lay person; (2) exhibits a certain level of autonomy in one's day-to-day conduct of professional practice; and (3) is guided by a code of ethics used to guide, educate, and discipline practitioners.
- **Donald Gotterbarn**, of East Tennessee State University, has argued that computer scientists have no business considering broad moral questions unless they directly affect practitioners in their industry.
- The **many hands problem** occurs when multiple hands are involved in the design, building, programming, and configuration of systems such as the iCloud servers or Therac-25; the issue makes it difficult to determine accountability.
- Some feel that accountability—and ethical behavior in general—is more achievable when there is **transparency**: that is, we behave better when we know we are being watched.
- A **whistleblower** is one who exposes, often at great risk to himself or herself, information or activity within an organization that he or she feels is illegal or unethical.
- University of Kansas professor and business ethicist Richard T. De George created a framework designed to determine when an employee is *permitted* to "blow the whistle" on a company practice, and when the employee is *obligated* to do so. The framework lists three criteria which, if met, would permit whistleblowing and an additional two criteria which, if met and combined with the first three, would make whistleblowing not only permitted, but obligatory.
- **Microethics** has to do with individuals and internal relations in the individuals' profession, while **macroethics** is more concerned with collective social responsibility and with broader societal decisions about technology.
- The primary goal of a free press is **objectivity**. News must be reported factually, with no slant, and must not be confused with opinion and analysis. However, this primary journalistic goal occasionally conflicts with an even more basic goal: the need to make money.
- In most states, a **shield law** protects reporters, shielding them from being forced to reveal sources, and in many states, this privilege has been recognized by the court. (The one state with no protection at all is Wyoming.)
- The thing about deepfakes and other misinformation is that they bring into play what is called the **liar's dividend**. People who really *did* say or do something can simply point to the evidence and call it a lie and be believed.
- Psychologists say that **FOMO** (Fear of Missing Out) may account for some of the addictive behavior we see exhibited by people who cannot bear to be unconnected.

- **Net neutrality** is the idea that internet service providers should allow all subscribers to access all content and applications regardless of the source, and without favoring or blocking particular products or websites, or charging different prices for specific types of content.
  - ◉ Proponents of net neutrality say that small companies will be squeezed out because they don't have the buying power to compete with the big service providers, and that all content should be accessible by all and for the same price.
  - ◉ Opponents of net neutrality believe that net neutrality is unfair, not only to some consumers, but also to the companies that must pay for the infrastructure on which the internet runs. Also, opponents believe that a so-called tiered internet will enable internet service providers to prioritize internet traffic, especially IoT traffic. This means that communications between medical devices or autonomous vehicles, for example, could be put in the fast lane. The opponents' base argument is that some internet services simply cost providers more and use up more of their bandwidth.
- **Cyberterrorism** is politically motivated hacking intended to result in loss of life, severe economic loss, or both.

Chapter 4

Ethics in Technology Post-Test

POST-TEST ANSWER SHEET

1. Ⓐ Ⓑ Ⓒ Ⓓ	18. Ⓐ Ⓑ Ⓒ Ⓓ	35. Ⓐ Ⓑ Ⓒ Ⓓ
2. Ⓐ Ⓑ Ⓒ Ⓓ	19. Ⓐ Ⓑ Ⓒ Ⓓ	36. Ⓐ Ⓑ Ⓒ Ⓓ
3. Ⓐ Ⓑ Ⓒ Ⓓ	20. Ⓐ Ⓑ Ⓒ Ⓓ	37. Ⓐ Ⓑ Ⓒ Ⓓ
4. Ⓐ Ⓑ Ⓒ Ⓓ	21. Ⓐ Ⓑ Ⓒ Ⓓ	38. Ⓐ Ⓑ Ⓒ Ⓓ
5. Ⓐ Ⓑ Ⓒ Ⓓ	22. Ⓐ Ⓑ Ⓒ Ⓓ	39. Ⓐ Ⓑ Ⓒ Ⓓ
6. Ⓐ Ⓑ Ⓒ Ⓓ	23. Ⓐ Ⓑ Ⓒ Ⓓ	40. Ⓐ Ⓑ Ⓒ Ⓓ
7. Ⓐ Ⓑ Ⓒ Ⓓ	24. Ⓐ Ⓑ Ⓒ Ⓓ	41. Ⓐ Ⓑ Ⓒ Ⓓ
8. Ⓐ Ⓑ Ⓒ Ⓓ	25. Ⓐ Ⓑ Ⓒ Ⓓ	42. Ⓐ Ⓑ Ⓒ Ⓓ
9. Ⓐ Ⓑ Ⓒ Ⓓ	26. Ⓐ Ⓑ Ⓒ Ⓓ	43. Ⓐ Ⓑ Ⓒ Ⓓ
10. Ⓐ Ⓑ Ⓒ Ⓓ	27. Ⓐ Ⓑ Ⓒ Ⓓ	44. Ⓐ Ⓑ Ⓒ Ⓓ
11. Ⓐ Ⓑ Ⓒ Ⓓ	28. Ⓐ Ⓑ Ⓒ Ⓓ	45. Ⓐ Ⓑ Ⓒ Ⓓ
12. Ⓐ Ⓑ Ⓒ Ⓓ	29. Ⓐ Ⓑ Ⓒ Ⓓ	46. Ⓐ Ⓑ Ⓒ Ⓓ
13. Ⓐ Ⓑ Ⓒ Ⓓ	30. Ⓐ Ⓑ Ⓒ Ⓓ	47. Ⓐ Ⓑ Ⓒ Ⓓ
14. Ⓐ Ⓑ Ⓒ Ⓓ	31. Ⓐ Ⓑ Ⓒ Ⓓ	48. Ⓐ Ⓑ Ⓒ Ⓓ
15. Ⓐ Ⓑ Ⓒ Ⓓ	32. Ⓐ Ⓑ Ⓒ Ⓓ	49. Ⓐ Ⓑ Ⓒ Ⓓ
16. Ⓐ Ⓑ Ⓒ Ⓓ	33. Ⓐ Ⓑ Ⓒ Ⓓ	50. Ⓐ Ⓑ Ⓒ Ⓓ
17. Ⓐ Ⓑ Ⓒ Ⓓ	34. Ⓐ Ⓑ Ⓒ Ⓓ	51. Ⓐ Ⓑ Ⓒ Ⓓ

52. Ⓐ Ⓑ Ⓒ Ⓓ   **55.** Ⓐ Ⓑ Ⓒ Ⓓ   **58.** Ⓐ Ⓑ Ⓒ Ⓓ

53. Ⓐ Ⓑ Ⓒ Ⓓ   **56.** Ⓐ Ⓑ Ⓒ Ⓓ   **59.** Ⓐ Ⓑ Ⓒ Ⓓ

54. Ⓐ Ⓑ Ⓒ Ⓓ   **57.** Ⓐ Ⓑ Ⓒ Ⓓ   **60.** Ⓐ Ⓑ Ⓒ Ⓓ

ETHICS IN TECHNOLOGY POST-TEST
72 minutes—60 questions

Directions: Carefully read each of the following 60 questions. Choose the best answer to each question and fill in the corresponding circle on the answer sheet. The Answer Key and Explanations can be found following this post-test.

---

1. One ethical concern about social media has to do with something called disinhibition. The term is used to describe

   A. what happens when personal data is collected by platforms and then sold to marketers.

   B. the collection of data by government agencies, which can then use that information to track you.

   C. the fact that, when data is sold and then resold, the source of that data loses track of its intended use.

   D. the tendency of people to say or do things anonymously that they would never say or do in person.

2. When discussing various aspects of cybersecurity, one must keep in mind three types of security: network security, system security, and

   A. legal security.

   B. physical security.

   C. data security.

   D. personal security

3. During the 2014 "Gamergate" controversy, a group of (mostly male) gamers, angry over perceived bias in gaming journalism that allegedly favored a group of (mostly female) gamers and game developers, used email, social networks, forum posts, and other online mechanisms to harass the female gamers. Threats included doxing and swatting. In the end, the attackers

   A. were arrested and received jail time.

   B. were served civil suits and had to pay reparations.

   C. were never apprehended, although much of the gaming industry came to the defense of the people being attacked.

   D. came forward and admitted they were in the wrong, promising to avoid such actions in the future.

4. One reason that Facebook has been accused of failing to police its platform is that

A. incidents of hate speech have increased dramatically over the past several years.

B. Facebook turns out to have made money by selling information about its subscribers.

C. the company failed to hire a Chief Privacy Officer.

D. there have been examples of people posting hate-filled rants on Facebook and then carrying out attacks that resulted in death or injuries.

5. While data mining is often seen in a negative light, it's important to keep in mind that it can be used for beneficial purposes. Which of the following purposes might NOT always be considered beneficial?

A. The discovery of human rights violations

B. The analysis of long-term weather patterns

C. The discovery of associations between individuals

D. The use of wireless sensor networks to monitor air pollution

6. The initial release of Google Glass, a form of AR (augmented reality) that involves the user wearing special glasses upon which information is displayed, was criticized by privacy-conscious users who felt that

A. its collection of user data via IR technology was a form of overreach.

B. it was too easy for Glass users to surreptitiously record people's activities.

C. the technology seemed poised to put thousands of people out of work.

D. the company's partnerships with credit agencies such as Equifax put users at risk.

7. If data can be used to distinguish a person's identity, or if it can be linked to data that can be used to identify a person, that data is classified as

A. PII

B. PDA

C. PET

D. PETA

8. In 2013, an NSA contract worker became a whistleblower, exposing a secret government surveillance program called PRISM. The worker was

A. Julian Assange.
B. Edward Snowden.
C. Chelsea (then Bradley) Manning.
D. Daniel Ellsberg.

9. The privacy of health data is a major concern for patients, physicians, and others. Which of the following is a federal law relating to the maintenance of that privacy?

A. FERPA
B. HIPAA
C. NCHS
D. PPA

10. The US National Security Agency (NSA) oversees a program that collects information from US internet companies. The NSA insists that it collects and examines only information about foreigners who might pose a threat to the United States. The program is called

A. Carnivore
B. Fairview
C. PRISM
D. Magic Lantern

11. A keylogger is

A. a middle-level manager whose job is to ensure that employees are at their desks and working.
B. software that captures keystrokes and communicates them to some surveillance apparatus.
C. software used to help users increase their typing speed.
D. a keyboard routine that logs keystrokes and tells users when their keyboards are due for replacement.

12. In October 2016, the FCC adopted a set of rules aimed at empowering consumers and enabling those consumers to determine how data is used and shared by internet service providers (ISPs) and requiring ISPs "to protect the privacy of their customers." In March 2017, that proposal was

    A. enacted into law and remains the broadest and most specific set of federal rules protecting internet consumers.
    B. "disapproved" by the United States House of Representatives and overturned, with President Donald Trump signing off on the proposal to negate these so-called net neutrality rules.
    C. overturned by the United States House of Representatives but saved by President Trump's veto of the House's actions.
    D. approved by the United States House of Representatives and signed into law by the president.

13. Which is said by privacy activists to have a more potentially negative effect: corporate data collection or government data collection?

    A. Corporate, because that sort of collection can affect your credit, your reputation, and work life
    B. Government, because the government has at its disposal much more power in terms of which data it can collect and how much
    C. Corporate, due to its sheer size and data-collection abilities
    D. Government, because it can restrict your liberty based on the data it collects

14. Company ABC collects massive amounts of unrelated and unstructured data and analyzes that data in order to spot business trends. What term is most often used to describe this process?

    A. Intrusive discovery
    B. Reactive business analysis
    C. Big data
    D. Relational database management

15. What have Facebook and its founder, Mark Zuckerberg, have been accused of disregarding in their zeal to commoditize information about the company's subscribers?

A. New technological innovations
B. Privacy concerns
C. The board of directors' profit goals
D. Anti-stalking laws

16. Some multinational companies might argue against "lawful access" because

A. it might give an unfair advantage to large companies that do business worldwide.
B. it could disadvantage small, up-and-coming companies run by entrepreneurs.
C. it gives police and intelligence agencies too much power at the expense of citizens' privacy.
D. people may be reluctant to purchase products or services from countries in which governments could have access to their private information.

17. In 2019, an organization known as ASVspoof.org sponsored an international challenge in which teams sought to

A. build a safer autonomous vehicle.
B. develop software to detect audio fakes.
C. locate and report on all URL spoofs.
D. find a way to help users avoid spoofed emails.

18. Many employers check applicants' social media posting before hiring—most even before interviewing. About half of the employers who check an applicant's social media postings are looking

A. to see if the applicant has a professional online persona.
B. for a reason not to hire the candidate.
C. to see if the applicant has any common connections with the interviewer or the company.
D. to see if they can find information that supports the candidate's claimed job qualifications.

19. The General Data Protection Regulation laws apply to companies doing business in

A. the United States.
B. the European Union.
C. Russia and the Baltic countries.
D. Scotland and Ireland.

20. The "Ten Commandments of Computer Ethics" (created in 1992 by members of the Computer Ethics Institute) are widely known and often quoted amongst technology ethicists and practitioners of the IT professions. But not everyone agrees with those commandments. Ben Fairweather, also of the Computer Ethics Institute, has criticized the "commandments" as being

A. impossible to follow.
B. unrealistic in this day and age.
C. too complicated to make sense, even to professionals.
D. simplistic and restrictive.

21. NSA contractor Edward Snowden was accused by the US Department of Justice of violating the Espionage Act of 1917, as well as theft of government property, when he leaked stolen NSA documents to the press in 2013. What country granted Snowden asylum?

A. Cuba
B. Russia
C. France
D. Puerto Rico

22. The 2013 Target credit card hack, which affected some 110 million customers, was ultimately found to have been caused by

A. credentials that had been stolen from the company's AC/HVAC vendor.
B. state actors believed to be in the employ of either Russia or North Korea.
C. a disgruntled employee who sold credentials to a hacker.
D. an employee who left a password on a Post-it note on a computer monitor.

23. Bots (automated user accounts or programs that post on user accounts) are estimated to create what percentage of tweets on the Twitter platform?

    A. More than 10%
    B. More than 25%
    C. More than 50%
    D. More than 75%

24. The spread of extremist ideology of all sorts has been attributed to social media, because

    A. the providers of such platforms are often in the vanguard of such ideologies, with many going so far as to identify themselves with extremism.
    B. social media provides a convenient communication mechanism that seems to amplify anger and distortions of all types.
    C. in many cases, the various platforms (Facebook, Twitter, etc.) have admitted contributing to the spread of extremism.
    D. that is the mechanism used by the majority of young people who wish to communicate.

25. The term "net neutrality" reflects the idea that

    A. websites and services should avoid political extremism and should offer neutral, objective, and factual views.
    B. internet sources, being, in effect, a public communications channel, ought not to support any particular political candidates.
    C. the internet should be governed by a neutral authority, such as the FCC.
    D. internet access should remain unfettered, and providers should not be able to provide "tiered" content—that is, charging different rates for different types of content.

26. In 2019, a 17-year-old high school dropout and two friends were arrested and accused of using social media to plan an attack on

    A. Islamberg, a Muslim settlement in upstate New York.
    B. a Jewish temple in White Plains, NY.
    C. a Christian church in southern Vermont.
    D. a Sikh temple in eastern Montana.

27. Many media analysts, including John G. Browning, an attorney and author of *The Lawyers Guide to Social Networking*, feel that legal complications have arisen in—or as a result of—social media largely because

    A. the various media outlets have refused to police their platforms.
    B. the law is unable to keep pace with rapid changes in technology.
    C. the law is biased against all forms of media.
    D. the media is biased against the law, which they see as restrictive.

28. Facebook and other social media platforms have played a large part in the spread of misinformation. Tech ethicists might call this

    A. a poor example of a tech-related issue.
    B. a solution to a common ethical issue.
    C. an example of a unique ethical issue.
    D. an exacerbation of an existing ethical issue.

29. PricewaterhouseCoopers (PwC) estimates that by 2020, some 30% of jobs will be

    A. entry-level.
    B. white collar.
    C. automated.
    D. "gig economy" jobs.

30. Facebook's stated policy is to ban "individuals or organizations that promote or engage in violence and hate, regardless of ideology." In the spring of 2019, the company removed several people from its platform, labeling them as "dangerous." The company removed all content from all of the following EXCEPT:

    A. Nation of Islam leader Louis Farrakhan
    B. *Infowars* host Alex Jones
    C. Fox News host Sean Hannity
    D. Conservative blogger/author Milo Yiannopoulos

31. A hacker who performs a break-in or hack in order to promote a political or social cause is known as a(n)

A. white-hat hacker.
B. hacktivist.
C. whistleblower.
D. social engineer.

32. The primary requirement of the press in a democratic society is that it be objective. That is, it must be factual and, insofar as possible, honest and objective. As for opinion,

A. there is no place for that in a free press.
B. it can be present, so long as it's clearly identifiable.
C. it cannot be on the same page as "straight news."
D. it can only be in the "Opinion" section.

33. The Islamic State's use of social media to recruit followers is an example of both cyberterrorism and

A. information warfare.
B. hacking.
C. hacktivism.
D. malicious Twitter bots.

34. In spite of First Amendment guarantees of free speech, the neo-Nazi blog, the *Daily Stormer*, was barred by GoDaddy, its original service provider, and then by Google, to which the blog had moved after being banned by GoDaddy. Shutting down the blog was legal because

A. hate speech is not allowed on the internet.
B. the *Daily Stormer* was in financial distress and had not paid its service bills.
C. both Google and GoDaddy are private companies and are free to censor as they wish.
D. while hate speech is allowed on the internet, obscenity is not, and both domain providers had determined that some of the blog's content was obscene.

35. The Association for Computing Machinery (ACM) Code of Ethics and Professional Conduct requires that members act responsibly, and that they follow other common sense principles. Which of the following is NOT one of those principles?

A. IT professionals must apologize for any harm they might inadvertently cause.

B. IT professionals must support the public good.

C. IT professionals must provide full disclosure of all system capabilities, limitations, and potential problems.

D. IT professionals must understand the responsibilities associated with the collection of personal information.

36. The Consumer Privacy Bill of Rights, a term used to describe a collection of legislative attempts to codify and regulate the processing of personal data in the United States,

A. became federal law in 2012.

B. was proposed and accepted by Congress and now awaits the president's signature.

C. would declare consumer privacy a basic American right.

D. was a California law passed in 2015; pending federal legislation is based upon that law.

37. There are no clear national or geographical boundaries in cyberspace, so

A. it is impossible to successfully prosecute someone for a criminal action.

B. jurisdictional issues make it difficult to track down and prosecute someone accused of a crime.

C. the NATO countries have banded together to ensure that criminals in any of those can be successfully prosecuted.

D. part of the EU charter guarantees that the members will cooperate when it comes to prosecuting crimes, including cybercrimes.

38. Cyberstalking is defined as the use of the internet to

    A. track down the home address of someone you've encountered on the internet.

    B. harass an individual or group.

    C. release someone's private information to members of an internet forum.

    D. demand money from someone you've met online in exchange for not releasing information about them.

39. What is the aim of international net neutrality?

    A. To impose limits on bandwidth based on type of content

    B. To ensure that international news aims for a neutral, factual, and objective presentation

    C. To ensure that not all content flowing through the internet is treated equally

    D. To ensure that internet content flows unimpeded and with equal access for all

40. A work that provides that the author retains residual rights, requiring the work be used "with permission" or under some form of license

    A. may nonetheless be in the public domain.

    B. cannot be considered to be in the public domain.

    C. can be licensed via the Creative Commons Attribution-Share Alike 2.0 Generic license in the public domain.

    D. cannot be used in any case by anyone other than the holder of those rights.

41. Encryption is a process by which

    A. data is hidden or made unreadable.

    B. hidden data is exposed and made readable.

    C. data is hidden by confusing or muddling the information.

    D. lost data is recovered.

42. "Doxing" someone—finding someone's publicly available information and posting it online—is generally considered to be

    A. illegal.

    B. legal.

    C. a harmless prank.

    D. something even the "victims" enjoy.

43. The General Data Protection Regulation (GDPR) is a set of data protection and privacy laws meant to protect the privacy of citizens. It was adopted in 2016 by whom?

A. The United States
B. Norway
C. The NATO Countries
D. The European Union

44. Material placed in the public domain

A. can be used only with permission of the author/publisher.
B. cannot be used in any commercial endeavor.
C. can be used only in commercial endeavors.
D. can be used freely for any purpose.

45. Distributed denial of service (DDoS) attacks are popular because they are effective and

A. simple to execute.
B. rarely leave clues as to the source of the attack.
C. don't cause any lasting damage to the target.
D. sophisticated.

46. An "immortalized" cell line is one that reproduces reliably and indefinitely and is thus valuable to researchers. One prominent (but unwitting) donor of such cells was

A. George Otto Gey.
B. Henrietta Lacks.
C. Charles Darwin.
D. John Moore.

47. In keeping with the results of the 1990 *Moore v. UCLA* lawsuit decision, most courts have subsequently found that

A. patients own their blood and tissue samples, and hospitals are not free to commercialize them without compensating the patient.
B. patients must sign a "donor form" in order to divest themselves of any commercial interest in their blood or tissue samples.
C. patients do not own their blood and tissue samples, and hospitals can commercialize them as they wish.
D. hospitals are free to use body tissues and blood samples, but not actual body parts, in commercialized research.

48. The internet began as ARPANET, a project run by

A. MIT

B. the US Department of Defense.

C. Sir Tim Berners-Lee.

D. Leonard Kleinrock, Vinton Cerf, Bob Kahn, and J.C.R. Licklider.

49. Dwight copies a 5-minute YouTube video and uploads it to his blog, where he writes a few sentences criticizing the video's author. Is this fair use?

A. Probably. Dwight is entitled to his opinion, and is allowed to use the video as evidence that his opinion is correct.

B. Probably not. Dwight used an entire video and only wrote a few sentences about it. That would probably violate the "amount and substantiality" test of "fair use."

C. Definitely. Dwight has the right to criticize the video.

D. Definitely not. Under no circumstances can Dwight upload and use an entire video.

50. The most widespread concern about IoT devices has to do with

A. expense.

B. security.

C. complexity.

D. agency.

51. In addition to deepfake videos, it is now possible to use artificial intelligence to create

A. word-for-word "language translators" for any domesticated animal.

B. audio that can speak any phrase in any voice with which it has been provided samples.

C. home computers more powerful than IBM's "Deep Blue" supercomputer.

D. Mars rovers programmed to speak in the language of any alien with which it might come into contact.

52. Stem cell research has been used to discover promising treatments and therapeutic avenues, but much debate has ensued, especially over the use of

    A. embryonic stem cells.
    B. adult stem cells.
    C. stolen stem cells.
    D. one's own stem cells.

53. Germany's Ethics Commission on Automated Driving recently issued what is probably the first set of guidelines for what it called "self-driving computers" (i.e., autonomous vehicles). Which of the following was NOT among the commission's recommendations or conclusions?

    A. Autonomous vehicles are necessary, as the systems cause fewer accidents than human drivers.
    B. Designers/programmers must not make any distinction between "personal features (age, gender, physical or mental constitution)" when making decisions in accident situations.
    C. Damage to property and damage to persons must be equally weighed and neither can take precedence over the other.
    D. Drivers must always be able to decide whether their vehicle data is forwarded and used.

54. Some ethicists have said that moral accountability is really very simple: we behave more ethically when we think we're being watched. If true, this means that corporations should ensure that their behavior is as

    A. transparent as possible.
    B. opaque as possible.
    C. professional as possible.
    D. correct as possible.

55. One of the ethical issues that arises when considering autonomous vehicles is the question of "data sovereignty." In the context of autonomous vehicles, data sovereignty means that

A. such vehicles are not allowed to collect data without each piece of data being approved by the driver.

B. drivers can decide whether data collected by the vehicle can be forwarded and used.

C. data collected by autonomous vehicles is inherently more valuable or important than data collected by other systems.

D. drivers must cede control of the data collected by their vehicles so that the vehicles and their designers can use the data to protect their lives and improve their systems.

56. The difference in the availability of technology among groups has been called the

A. digital divide.

B. equity gap.

C. gender gap.

D. logic gap.

57. The (1996) Computer Fraud and Abuse Act (CFAA) outlaws various types of online fraud, including trafficking in what?

A. Illicit drugs

B. Stolen artifacts

C. Personally identifiable information

D. Passwords

58. Wilneida Negrón, a Technology Fellow at the Ford Foundation, has identified several trends that she believes will impact social justice issues over the next few years. One of those issues is the need for increased digital privacy rights. In discussing that issue, she noted a recent Supreme Court ruling in *Carpenter v. United States*. That case concerned

A. students' right to use phones in the classroom.

B. government access to cellular location data.

C. the fact that the Constitution specifically promises citizens a right to privacy.

D. cellular service providers noting the location of phone owners.

59. In "celebgate," hackers broke into Apple's iCloud storage and stole nude photos of celebrities. In that instance, one could NOT reasonably hold which of the following responsible?

    A. The hacker(s)
    B. Apple Computer Corporation
    C. Apple engineers and programmers
    D. The celebrities involved

60. Law professors Robert Chesney and Danielle Keats Citron have studied the phenomenon of "deepfakes" and the possible impacts of such technology. What is a "deepfake"?

    A. A lie uttered often enough to convince the majority of listeners
    B. A fake technology, sometimes referred to as "vaporware"
    C. Technology that allows the creation of realistic fake videos of people
    D. Any misinformation spread via a social media platform

ANSWER KEY AND EXPLANATIONS

1. D	13. D	25. D	37. B	49. B
2. C	14. C	26. A	38. B	50. B
3. C	15. B	27. B	39. D	51. B
4. D	16. D	28. D	40. B	52. A
5. C	17. B	29. C	41. A	53. C
6. B	18. A	30. C	42. B	54. A
7. A	19. B	31. B	43. D	55. B
8. B	20. D	32. B	44. D	56. A
9. B	21. B	33. A	45. A	57. D
10. C	22. A	34. C	46. B	58. B
11. B	23. B	35. A	47. C	59. D
12. B	24. B	36. C	48. B	60. C

1. **The correct answer is D.** Disinhibition is the term sociologists use to describe the tendency of people hiding behind a cloak of anonymity—or simply encouraged by their online friends—to say and do hateful, confrontational, or insulting things. Personal data is indeed collected and sold to marketers (choice A), and one does eventually lose track of it and its possible use (choice C), but disinhibition is not the term used to describe that phenomenon. Government agencies can and do view online information (choice B), but disinhibition is not the term used to describe that activity.

2. **The correct answer is C.** The third type of security has to do with ensuring that private data is kept private or is shared only with those whom one wishes to share it. There are certainly legal issues involved (choice A), but legal issues themselves do not constitute a type of security. Similarly, your personal and/or physical security (choice B) are of great importance, but are rarely put at risk; with a few exceptions, one's physical or personal security (choice D) is normally not what we mean when we talk about the three types of cybersecurity.

3. **The correct answer is C.** While the gaming industry came to the defense of the people being attacked, the attackers were never all identified, and therefore were not apprehended. No charges or lawsuits were filed and the perpetrators never apologized.

4. **The correct answer is D.** There have been Facebook posts (often antisemitic or anti-Muslim) by attackers who ultimately killed or injured people. In most cases, the posts remained up until after the attacks. The number of hate speech incidents (choice A) has certainly increased, but it would be difficult—and unfair—to lay that at the feet of any one social media platform. Facebook (and other social media platforms) didn't "turn out" to have made money by selling such information (choice B); that *is* in fact how they make money—they sell (anonymized) information about their users to marketers. The company does have a Chief Privacy Officer (choice C): Erin Egan, a former lawyer who specialized in privacy and data security.

5. **The correct answer is C.** Of all the choices, only choice C is likely to be misused. While collection of such data could lead to finding members of, say, a terrorist cell, it could also be exploited by authoritarian governments seeking to establish a sort of "guilt by association" based on tracking and profiling "friends-of-friends-of-friends." The other choices describe benign or even helpful uses of data mining.

6. **The correct answer is B.** Google Glass includes video-recording technology that can be activated without the knowledge of those being recorded. Google Glass did not utilize IR (infrared) technology (choice A), and, although people often worry about new technologies putting people out of work (choice C), that was not the case here. As far as we know, Google has not partnered with credit-reporting agencies (choice D); in any case, there was no connection between Google Glass and such agencies.

7. **The correct answer is A.** PII (or personally identifiable information) is data that can be used to trace someone's identity, directly or indirectly. A PDA (choice B) is a personal digital assistant, a tool generally superseded these days by smart phones. A PET (choice C) is a privacy-enhancing tool, such as Anonymizer or TrackMeNot, that can be used in a web browser to obfuscate one's identity and the source of a query. PETA (choice D) is People for the Ethical Treatment of Animals, an animal rights group.

8. The correct answer is B. Snowden leaked the details of PRISM, a multi-agency surveillance program under which the US government collects communications from various internet companies. The government states that the program targets only foreigners, but the ACLU and other groups have accused the government of spying on US citizens. Julian Assange (choice A) founded WikiLeaks, a publishing organization that published leaks provided by former US Army soldier Chelsea Manning (choice C). Ellsberg (choice D) was a military analyst who leaked the Pentagon Papers in 1971.

9. The correct answer is B. HIPAA is the Health Insurance Portability and Accountability Act, which addresses the potential breaching of personally identifiable information (PII), among other things. FERPA (choice A) is the Family Educational Rights and Privacy Act; it does address privacy, among other things, but not as relates to health records. The NCHS (choice C) is the National Center for Health Statistics, and the PPA (choice D) is the Prompt Payment Act, which specifies that the federal government is to pay its vendors promptly.

10. The correct answer is C. The existence of PRISM was leaked in 2013 by NSA contractor Edward Snowden. Carnivore (choice A) was an FBI program designed to monitor electronic communications; it has apparently been replaced by commercial software. Fairview (choice B) is a mass surveillance program aimed at foreigners and overseen by the NSA in which phone, internet, and email data is collected from AT&T. Magic Lantern (choice D) is an FBI keystroke logging program that is deployed via email.

11. The correct answer is B. A keylogger (such as that deployed by the FBI's Magic Lantern program) logs users' keystrokes and sends them off to be deciphered/analyzed by someone. There are managers whose job it is to ensure that employees are working (choice A), but they are not called keyloggers. A keylogger could be used to measure one's typing speed (choice C), but that is not generally its purpose. Your keyboard (choice D) will tell you when it's due to be replaced by failing—usually at the worst possible moment.

12. **The correct answer is B.** The rules originally approved in 2016 were overturned by the House in 2017. The original rules were lobbied against by ISPs and other providers. The rules were "disapproved" before they were enacted into law, so choices A and D cannot be correct. Though the house overturned the proposal, choice C erroneously indicates that President Trump reversed this decision.

13. **The correct answer is D.** Companies might collect a great deal of data about you, but corporations can't take specific actions that restrict your liberties. The government, on the other hand, can prosecute and even jail you. It's true that corporate data collection can affect your credit (choice A), but that's not as bad as being jailed. It's also true that the government has more data-collecting power (choice B) than corporations, but the real danger, say privacy activists, is that the government has the power to use that data to restrict your liberty. Corporate data-gathering resources (choice C), though impressive, are no match for a government's ability to utilize multiple agencies' personnel and technology in its data-collection efforts.

14. **The correct answer is C.** This is the definition of big data: the collection and analysis of huge sets of often unrelated and unstructured data. The analysis may discover information and it (or the use to which it is put) may turn out to be intrusive (choice A), but that is not what the process is called. If anything, the process tends to be proactive, rather than reactive, as choice B erroneously indicates. Standard relational database management software (choice D) is generally not powerful or sophisticated enough to analyze the massive amounts and types of data collected during this process.

15. **The correct answer is B.** The company has recently pledged an "about face" in its seeming disregard for subscribers' privacy, but the effectiveness of that pledge remains to be seen. In the meantime, the company has done a poor job of protecting users' privacy, even though the main purpose of the platform is to share information about people (with most of that information being placed online by the very people using the service). Choice A is incorrect because Facebook stays quite current when it comes to new technology, regularly utilizing such things as AI, facial recognition, and more—often, however, to the detriment of users' privacy, which is part of the issue. Choice C doesn't make sense as the company's board should have no complaints about the company's profitability. In spite of privacy scandals, Facebook's *profit* (not gross revenue) for the 4th quarter of 2019 was almost $7 billion. Facebook has not been accused of disregarding stalking laws (choice D), although some of its users may have been "stalking" others. Keep in mind that Section 230 of the Communications Decency Act provides ISPs with immunity from liability for what others publish on their services.

16. **The correct answer is D.** If a company does business in China, for example, it might be reluctant to continue doing business there, because the government (and possibly competing Chinese companies) might have access to its trade secrets. Such a law would not give an advantage to large companies as choice A indicates. Choice B doesn't make much sense as a large company probably would not care much about the fortunes of newer, smaller companies. Some people at the multinational companies might worry individually about an abuse of government power at the expense of citizens' privacy, but choice C is not the best answer because the companies as a whole would likely not.

17. **The correct answer is B.** Various companies, organizations, and government entities are attempting to use artificial intelligence or other means to detect and report on "fake audios" that represent someone (often a politician or celebrity) making statements that he or she never actually made. The other three choices all represent laudable efforts, many of them ongoing, but ASVspoof.org was organized specifically to learn how to detect fake audio.

18. **The correct answer is A.** Many interviewers and HR departments check applicants' social media posts, and the most common reason for checking is to determine if the applicant has a "professional" online persona. That doesn't mean that they're looking for professional dress or industry connections; it simply means they check to see if there are drinking- or drug-related photos or anything distasteful about the applicant's posts. In addition, while employers may be tempted to look for reasons *not* to hire the candidate (due possibly from the excessive amounts of resumes submitted for the position), this reason is more a justification, rather than an initial reason to check social media.

19. **The correct answer is B.** Companies located in—or doing business in—Europe are subject to the provisions of GDPR. None of the other countries are affected, unless they happen to do business with EU companies or EU residents.

20. **The correct answer is D.** Fairweather criticizes many of the "commandments," noting, for example, that the commandment prescribing that professionals must "think about the social consequences" of their programs is much too simplistic. He says, "Thought, unaccompanied by action, is pointless. They must act upon those thoughts." Fairweather further notes, ". . . just because you keep within the ten commandments does not mean that what you are doing is OK . . . . Additionally, some of the 'ten commandments' appear to be decidedly trivial compared to the others: yet the listing suggests that all ten are equally important."

21. **The correct answer is B.** Snowden was at first required to stay in Moscow's Sheremetyevo Airport, but eventually Russia granted him asylum, extending his visa several times until finally granting him permanent asylum in October 2020. Cuba (choice A) has in the past granted asylum to US citizens (including CIA officer Philip Agee and activist Eldridge Cleaver), but it did not offer asylum to Snowden. France (choice C) was not involved in the affair, and Puerto Rico (choice D) is not a country, but a US territory.

22. **The correct answer is A.** Often the route into a hacking target is indirect; in this case, hackers did not need to steal log-in credentials from Target itself, they simply stole them from a (much easier to breach) vendor. This is often how hacks occur. In this case, state actors (choice B) were not involved, nor was a disgruntled employee (choice C). An employee may in fact have had a password taped to or stuck on a monitor (choice D)—many do, in spite of warnings not to. In this case, however, that is not how entry was gained.

23. **The correct answer is B.** Twitter bots are estimated to create about 25% of Twitter content. Keep in mind that not all of that bot-created content is negative or misinformative. Most of it is valid content that follows the rules for bot behavior laid down by Twitter.

24. **The correct answer is B.** Social media is a convenient—and incredibly efficient—communicative mechanism, and it seems to amplify extreme views, perhaps because of the disinhibition of those using it; it's simply easier to say hateful things when safely hidden behind a digital wall of anonymity. The people behind Facebook and the like (choice A) have made great efforts to distance themselves from the extreme language often found on their sites, and few if any would admit (choice C) to having contributed. Social media is certainly the mechanism used by the majority of young people to communicate (choice D), but that doesn't mean that this is the reason for an increase in extremism—after all, billions of people use social media and do not become extremists.

25. **The correct answer is D.** Supporters of net neutrality argue that the internet is essentially a public utility, and providers should not be able to charge different rates for different types of content; in effect, say supporters, that would be "playing favorites." The term has nothing to do with the idea that content providers should remain neutral in some form, as choices A and C erroneously indicate. Note that, to some extent, the FCC actually does regulate the internet (though not its content or privacy), and it was, in fact the FCC that in 2018 repealed rules that barred providers from blocking, slowing, or prioritizing internet content.

26. **The correct answer is A.** Islamberg is a Muslim community in Delaware County, NY. Vincent Vetromile, a young man in Rochester, NY, was accused of planning a violent attack, using guns and explosive devices, on the Muslim enclave. The other choices were not targets in this attack, though Jewish temples (choice B), Christian churches (choice C), and Sikh temples (choice D) have all been attacked.

27. **The correct answer is B.** Browning and others feel that social media complications—issues such as jurors accessing the internet during deliberations and posting Facebook polls to find out how they should vote on a case—have arisen largely because the law has not kept up with the pace of technological change. While the media platforms have in many cases refused—or been unable—to police posted content, choice A is not the best answer because that is not what Browning and others say is at the root of the problem. Neither the law (choice C) nor the media (choice D) are being accused of bias.

28. **The correct answer is D.** The fact that social media platforms have played a large part in the spread of misinformation is an example of an exacerbated issue. Misinformation has always existed, and it has always been spread, whether by newspapers, radio, word-of-mouth, or by other means. Now, however, technology has democratized misinformation: anyone can spread it, further and more quickly than ever before. The opposite of choice A is true; this is a very good example of a tech-related ethical issue. The spread of misinformation is a serious ethical issue—not a solution to an issue as choice B erroneously indicates. Choice C is incorrect because the issue is not unique or new; misinformation has always existed and has always been spread by various means.

29. The correct answer is C. PwC estimates that 30% or more of jobs worldwide could be automated by 2020. Ethicists say this implies that retraining and re-education should be readily available for those whose jobs have disappeared. Entry-level jobs (choice A) were not considered separately by PwC. It may be true that the percentage of white-collar jobs is increasing (choice B), since it's blue-collar jobs that tend to get automated first, but the PwC report did not say that 30% will be entry-level. "Gig economy" jobs (choice D) are often temporary and/or flexible and have become more prevalent. However, the PwC did not say that they will account for 30% by 2020. But a 2018 Gallup poll estimated that nearly that percentage of jobs are *currently* gig economy jobs.

30. The correct answer is C. Fox News host Sean Hannity was not removed. The other media personalities and activists listed were removed after Facebook had "reevaluated the content that they had posted previously, or had examined their activities outside of Facebook," the company said.

31. The correct answer is B. Hacktivism is the act of performing a hack in order to promote a cause. A white-hat hacker (choice A) is one who works for a government or corporate entity, and who, under their auspices, breaks into protected systems in order to test their security. A whistleblower (choice C) could also be a hacker, but the term is more generally used to describe someone who exposes organizational information or behavior deemed to be illegal or unethical. A social engineer (choice D) is someone who uses psychology and trickery to manipulate people unto giving up secrets—often passwords or network credentials.

32. The correct answer is B. So long as opinion is clearly identified as such, it can certainly exist in a newspaper, a broadcast, a blog, etc. Choice A doesn't make sense as opinion is a valuable component of the press, and a tool that's useful in helping readers, listeners, or viewers understand and determine how they feel about a news item. To say it cannot be on the "same page" as straight news (choice C) is incorrect, since there might be opinion in an analysis piece or a sidebar. Again, as long as it's identified as opinion, that is perfectly acceptable. Certainly, we can assume that everything in the "Opinion" section is opinion (choice D), but that is not the only place we might find evidence of a writer's (or the publisher's) opinion.

33. The correct answer is A. Information warfare is the use of weaponized information to create a strategic or tactical advantage. Generally, it is thought to include the notion that the target is unaware that the information being received has been manipulated. Hacking (choice B), hacktivism (choice C), and malicious Twitter bots (choice D) are used in information warfare, not as social media recruitment tools for the Islamic State.

34. The correct answer is C. Private companies are free to regulate free speech on their platforms. Generally, hate speech is allowed on the internet (choice A), until and unless the provider deems otherwise. The blog's financial situation (choice B) had no bearing on its removal from the two domains. The blog was not accused of publishing obscenity (choice D), which in any case, is not always illegal. For example, creating and watching adult pornography is legal; creating or watching child pornography is not.

35. The correct answer is A. You do not need to know the specific content of the code to recognize that merely apologizing for harm done is not enough, which is why the code actually says that the programmer must take steps to *mitigate* any inadvertent harm done. The other choices accurately, though incompletely, reflect some of the principles of the ACM Code of Ethics and Professional Conduct.

36. **The correct answer is C.** The Consumer Privacy Bill of Rights would declare privacy a basic right. So far, though, none of the proposed laws related to this "bill" have become law, so it was not enacted in 2012 (choice A). The "bill" was not accepted by Congress (choice B), and the "bill" is not a California law passed in 2015 (choice D).

37. **The correct answer is B.** Because the alleged criminal may live in one jurisdiction and the victim(s) in another, and since the data involved in the crime (emails, messages, transactions, etc.) may travel through servers in any of several countries, it is difficult to establish the jurisdiction in which the crime took place, let alone the one in which it should be prosecuted. It's not impossible to prosecute a cybercrime (choice A), just sometimes very difficult. Neither the NATO countries (choice C) nor the EU (choice D) have worked together to guarantee cooperation when it comes to prosecuting cybercrimes.

38. **The correct answer is B.** Cyberstalking is using the internet to harass or stalk an individual. There's nothing illegal about using the internet to track down someone's address (choice A); it's what you do with that information that could constitute cyberstalking. Releasing someone's private information (choice C) is called doxing; it may be a part of a pattern of cyberstalking, but is not in itself cyberstalking. Demanding money from someone in exchange for not divulging potentially damaging or private information (choice D) is extortion, not cyberstalking.

39. **The correct answer is D.** Net neutrality (international or otherwise) is the idea that all content should be accessible to all, and that providers cannot charge different rates for different types of content. Limiting bandwidth based on content type (choice A) is actually what net neutrality argues against, as is the idea that content should not be treated (and charged for) equally (choice C). Net neutrality has nothing to do with neutral, factual, and objective presentations of content (choice B).

40. **The correct answer is B.** If the work is offered under any form of license including a Creative Commons license, then it is not truly in the public domain. This eliminates choices A and C as viable answers. Choice D goes too far to say that the work simply cannot be used in any case by anyone. What if the license holder grants permission? What if the user meets some other provision of the license? Many IP items offered under the Creative Commons license simply require a "permission by" credit and perhaps a link to the Creative Commons license language.

41. **The correct answer is A.** Encryption is the term used to describe several processes by which data is hidden or scrambled such that it cannot be read. Choice B describes decryption. Choice C describes obfuscation. Note, though, that if the information is confused enough—or surrounded by other data meant to mislead the reader—then it might as well be encrypted, since it cannot be discovered. The process by which lost data is recovered (choice D) is simply called recovery or restoration.

42. **The correct answer is B.** So-called doxing (from "docs" or documents") is often perfectly legal—depending on the circumstances and the results. However, even when the act itself is legal, the precursors to the act (how the data was obtained) and the consequences of the act (potential harassment, invasion of privacy, intimidation, etc.) may not be. If someone uses illegal means, such as hacking, to obtain the data, that in itself is illegal (choice A), and so is any use to which that data is put. If the victim is harmed by the act, that can constitute intimidation, assault, or an invasion of privacy (choice C). Doxing can also constitute a form of cyberstalking. (After all, the whole point of doxing someone is usually to cause the victim to suffer negative consequences.) Note that doxing is not harmless, and victims do not enjoy having their information exposed (choice D); if they wanted that information known, they would have published it themselves.

43. **The correct answer is D.** The EU member-states passed the GDPR, which provides protection for the data and privacy of citizens of its members. The United States (choice A) is not a member of the EU and did not pass the GDPR, although there are some US laws that attempt to provide for the privacy of its citizens. Norway (choice B) is not a member of the EU, and the 29 NATO countries (choice C), while each has its own privacy laws, did not pass the GDPR.

44. **The correct answer is D.** Material placed in (or which has reverted to) the public domain is free for use. No exclusive IP rights apply to such creative works. One does not need the permission of the author or publisher (choice A) to use public domain works (this often—but not always—includes works created under government auspices), and it does not matter whether the use is commercial or nonprofit (choices B and C).

45. **The correct answer is A.** DDoS attacks are simple, straightforward, and easy to execute. All you need is some code that will send repeated requests to the target; send enough requests and the server will be inundated and unable to respond to legitimate requests. The result is that no one can contact that server or get on that website. The opposite of choice B is true. DDoS attacks actually do leave clues as to the origin of the attack, although there are ways to obfuscate that location. Choice C is not the best answer because while DDoS attacks don't generally cause any physical damage, rendering a commercial website or ecommerce site unavailable can cost a company many thousands—or even millions—of dollars. Choice D is incorrect because a DDoS attack is not sophisticated at all; that's part of its appeal.

46. The correct answer is B. The cells of Henrietta Lacks, a cancer patient at Johns Hopkins, were cultured and studied, and eventually used without her knowledge or consent as tools for research and treatment. Lacks died in 1951 and never knew of her unwitting contribution to medical science. George Otto Gey (choice A) is the researcher who cultured Lacks' cells. Charles Darwin (choice C) was not a donor (wittingly or otherwise) of cells. John Moore (choice D) is a leukemia patient who filed suit in 1976 after his cell line was commercialized by a UCLA physician. Moore lost his suit.

47. The correct answer is C. The California Supreme Court and other US courts have determined that patients do not own the blood or tissue samples taken from their bodies (thus, choice A is incorrect). Patients do not need to sign a donor form, because they're already divested of interest (choice B), according to the courts. The courts made no distinction between blood and tissue samples and actual body parts (choice D).

48. The correct answer is B. The Advanced Research Projects Agency Network (ARPANET) was created under the auspices of the US Department of Defense. MIT (choice A) was an early participant in the project. Sir Tim Berners-Lee (choice C) is an internet pioneer who invented the browser and the HTML markup language used to link one web document to another, but that did not occur until 1990. The four men in choice D were indeed all early internet pioneers, but they did not run ARPANET.

49. The correct answer is B. Dwight can't use an entire work and call it "fair use," especially when that entire work (the video, in this case) is significantly larger than your contribution. Dwight's few sentences have not "transformed" the work into something original, and the total size of the "new" work is not much larger or longer than the original video. Dwight might be able to use part of the video to bolster his opinion (choice A), but probably not the whole thing; he can criticize the video, but the preponderance of the final work must be his. It's difficult to say "definitely" about anything related to the law (choice C). There may be circumstances in which Dwight could use the whole video (choice D): Perhaps the video itself is in the public domain. Perhaps Dwight's analysis is much longer and more complex than the video. Perhaps he has permission from the holder of the video's copyright. You would be wise to mistrust any answers that include the terms "definitely," always," or "never."

50. The correct answer is B. Small devices in your home or office are inherently insecure—they simply don't have the sophisticated operating systems that work to protect larger, more complex devices, such as our computers. The bottom line is that it's easy to break into most IoT devices; they're vulnerable, and since they're connected to your network, the network is also vulnerable. Expense (choice A) is not really an issue; these items (and the infrastructures through which they communicate) have become very affordable. IoT devices tend not to be particularly complex (choice C); in fact, their simplicity often presents a security risk, as noted in choice B. Agency (choice D)—or more accurately, a loss of agency—is definitely an issue, but not the foremost or most publicized one. In fact, it's rarely discussed: The fear is that we lose the ability to make decisions when statisticians study large groups of data and use that info to predict our behavior, feelings, and thoughts. That is, we lose agency, the ability to wield power over our own lives.

51. **The correct answer is B.** Audio deepfakes have reached the point where the program can speak any phrase in any specific voice, thus making it appear as if that person actually uttered the phrase or sentence. We cannot yet translate your dog's bark or your cat's purr (choice A), nor any other animal's native language. Artificial intelligence has not (yet) been harnessed and made available in a form that would allow a home computer to outperform IBM's "Deep Blue" chess-playing computer (choice C), which defeated reigning chess champion Garry Kasparov in 1997. Finally, we don't know any alien languages—if there are any—so it's not possible for a program to speak in those languages (choice D).

52. **The correct answer is A.** The use of embryonic stem cells is fraught with debate, the ethical issue being that such use can destroy the embryo. Since an embryo can develop into a human being—and since many consider that the embryo is already a human being—such research is highly controversial. The debate over the use of adult stem cells (choice B) is much more muted, since the destruction of an embryo is not involved, as is the use of one's own stem cells (choice D). The idea of stolen stem cells (choice C) has not become part of the debate.

53. **The correct answer is C.** The commission determined that in hazardous situations, the protection of life must have priority. All of the other choices reflect elements of the commission's recommendations.

54. **The correct answer is A.** Transparency means that others can see the actions we perform. This encourages openness and accountability. Opaque (choice B) means the opposite of transparent, while being professional (choice C) does not always equate to being either ethical or transparent. It's not enough to be correct (choice D): A computer can calculate that if your autonomous vehicle must crash into someone, it should injure the fewest people. According to the program, that is the "correct" calculation, but one can argue forever over whether it is the "right" action to take. As HPE's Dr. Eng Lim Goh has noted, ". . . while machines are increasingly relied on to make correct decisions, we need to be there to make sure that it is also the right decision. What's correct may not always be right. We are the last judge."

55. **The correct answer is B.** Data sovereignty has to do with who is control of data. The vehicle must collect data in order to function, but according to the principle of data sovereignty, the driver/owner should be in control of what happens to the data afterward. Data is collected and analyzed at such a rapid pace that there is no way for a user to view and approve each piece of data as it is collected (choice A). There is nothing that makes vehicular data more valuable than data collected by your other systems (choice C), including your phone, computer, smart home, etc. The idea behind data sovereignty is that the driver must *not* be forced to cede control (choice D).

56. **The correct answer is A.** The digital divide (also known as the technology gap) has to do with the fair and equitable availability of technology to groups of people. If one group has access and another does not, then the latter group is at a social and economic disadvantage. None of the other choices reflects the term used to describe that difference in availability.

57. **The correct answer is D.** The CFAA outlaws trafficking in (presumably stolen) passwords. It does not address trafficking in illicit drugs (choice A), stolen artifacts (choice B), or PII—personally identifiable information (choice C).

58. **The correct answer is B.** The case revolved around the government use of cellular geotracking and acquisition of a cell customer's data; the Court held that "an individual maintains a legitimate expectation of privacy in the record of his physical movements as captured through" a cell phone. The case had nothing to do with students in the classroom (choice A). Nowhere does the Constitution specifically guarantee a right to privacy (choice C). The Fourth Amendment, however, does guarantee protection against unreasonable searches and seizures; in some cases, this has been interpreted to imply a measure of protection of one's privacy. Providers track the locations of phones simply as a matter of providing service. In addition, if you want your mapping (and some other) applications to work, the providers must be able to track the location of your phone (choice D). The issue revolved around government access to that data.

59. **The correct answer is D.** The celebrities actually erased the data from their phones, but not from the iCloud servers. One might argue that they should have known to do so, but the fact is that the notion of data sovereignty means that they own that data and should have been in a secure position, having entrusted that data to a cloud service; the fact that they were not was not their fault. The hackers (choice A), obviously, committed the crime. But many have argued that Apple itself (choice B) should have done a better job of securing the data it holds for its customers, and that individual engineers (choice C) should have either done a better job securing the data or should have notified Apple (and/or the public) that the data's security was in question.

60. **The correct answer is C.** New technology allows us to create fake videos and audio of people seemingly doing and saying things they did not say or do in real life. These deepfakes (sometimes rendered as "deep fakes") are then spread via social media. An oft-uttered lie (choice A) is simply one that is repeated many times—an effective technique, as many dictators and others have found. Vaporware (choice B) is software that never made it to market—and was perhaps never intended to. Not all misinformation is a deepfake (choice D), though all deepfakes are by definition misinformation.

9 780768 944471